OUR SPORTS HERITAGE

Herder Memorial
TROPHY

*A History of Senior Hockey
in Newfoundland and Labrador*

BILL ABBOTT

BREAKWATER
100 Water Street
P.O. Box 2188
St. John's, NF
A1C 6E6

Cover photograph courtesy of The Telegram.
Herder Memorial Trophy photograph by Don Meiwald.

Interior photographs courtesy The Telegram.

Canadian Cataloguing in Publication Data

Abbott, Bill, 1950-

    Herder Memorial Trophy

    (Our sports heritage)

    ISBN 1-55081-156-8

1. Herder Memorial Trophy — History.   2. Hockey — Newfoundland —
History.   I. Title.   II. Series.

GV848.4.C3A22 2000   796.962'609718   C00-95022-7

Copyright © 2000 Breakwater Books Ltd.

ALL RIGHTS RESERVED. No part of this work covered by the copyright hereon
may be reproduced or used in any form or by any means—graphic, elec-
tronic or mechanical—without the prior written permission of the publisher. Any request for photocopying, recording, taping or storing in an
information retrieval system of any part of this book shall be directed in
writing to the Canadian Reprography Collective, 6 Adelaide Street East,
Suite 900, Toronto, Ontario, M5C 1H6. This applies to classroom usage as
well.

Canadä   We acknowledge the financial support of the Government
of Canada through the Book Publishing Industry
Development Program (BPIDP) for our publishing activities.

PRINTED IN CANADA.

Acknowledgements

The concept **Our Sports Heritage** became an idea many years ago. Throughout my career as a sportswriter and my involvement as an amateur sports administrator, I have realized the need for our sports heritage to be preserved for the many generations to follow. The history of sport and the impact it has had on communities in Newfoundland and Labrador has been tremendous.

It was through the vision of publisher Clyde Rose of Breakwater Books Ltd. that this concept has become a reality. This is the first volume of many in the **Our Sports Heritage** collection which will highlight the athletic achievements of our athletes and depict the social and cultural effect sport has had on the lives of our people.

Many people have played a role in the culmination of this first volume. A great number of former players have assisted in the research, through interviews and stories about the glory days of senior hockey in this province. The staffs at the Newfoundland section of the A. C. Hunter library and the provincial sports archives deserve a special thank you for their co-operation on the many occasions they assisted me in my research.

The Newfoundland and Labrador Hockey Association celebrates its 65th anniversary this year and I have been fortunate to have been a part of the provincial senior hockey scene for over 30 years as a reporter and a referee. My love for the game has been instrumental in selecting The Herder Memorial Trophy as the first book in the series.

The senior hockey players who have graced us with their fine play and entertainment for the past 65 years deserve a special mention and a thank you for providing spectators throughout the province with first class entertainment during the long Newfoundland winters.

— *Bill Abbott*

MESSAGE FROM THE MINISTER OF
TOURISM, CULTURE AND RECREATION

As the Minister responsible for sport and recreation in the province, I am pleased to join with you in paying tribute to the Herder Memorial Trophy, a longstanding tradition in our sports community.

Hockey has been an integral part of the sport scene in the province for many years. From ponds and back yards to rinks and stadiums, many generations of Newfoundlanders and Labradorians have loved a good game of hockey.

Our Provincial Senior Hockey League has always been a force to be reckoned with, providing excitement and entertainment for generation after generation. We take our game of hockey very seriously, and Newfoundland and Labrador has consequently produced numerous athletes of international calibre. From the time they are able to put on their first pair of skates, young men and women have developed a passion for the game. The Herder Memorial Trophy has long been a measure of excellence, as thousands have relentlessly pursued this prestigious and coveted prize, since its debut in 1935. It is truly an icon of the sports culture in the province.

I would like to congratulate Breakwater, the publisher of this special publication, which pays a fitting and well-deserved tribute to the Herder Memorial Trophy. May this valued tradition be a *goal* for generations of hockey players to come!

CHARLES FUREY

On behalf of the Newfoundland and Labrador Hockey Association, I want to extend sincere congratulations to Breakwater Books on the introduction of Our Sports Heritage collection and for selecting the history of the Herder Memorial Trophy as your initial book in the series.

Senior hockey in Newfoundland and Labrador has had a very proud tradition since its inception in 1935 and continues to grow today. I am sure this series will truly reflect the part that senior hockey has played in the lives of so many people in this province.

The Newfoundland and Labrador Hockey Association is celebrating its 65th. anniversary this year and it is fitting that the first book on the history of the Herder Memorial Trophy will play a role in our celebrations and the opening of our Hockey Hall of Fame in Corner Brook.

Sincerely,

George Fardy,
President

The

St. John's Maple Leafs

are proud to play

a role in sharing

Newfoundland and Labrador's

culture and sports heritage

and are proud to be a

sponsor of the first edition of

OUR SPORTS HERITAGE.

Contents

CONGRATULATIONS

on

OUR SPORTS HERITAGE

from

THE PEOPLE'S PAPER

The Telegram

Proud Sponsor

of

The Herder Memorial Trophy

and

The Telegram Trophy

www.thetelegram.com

Introduction

When the Corner Brook Royals boarded the train in March of 1935 for a 32-hour trip to St. John's to play the Guards for the inaugural Newfoundland senior hockey championship, they had no idea that this this inauspicious two-game series for the Herder Memorial Trophy would propel senior hockey in Newfoundland and Labrador into the limelight as one of the premier sporting events in the province's history. The idea for providing a series to determine a true Newfoundland champion was born from a letter to the editor of the Evening Telegram from a hockey fan in Bay Roberts. The Rovers had just captured the Conception Bay championship and the writer suggested a series between the Bay Roberts sextet and the Guards, the St. John's Boyle Trophy champions, for the title.

The Telegram donated a trophy named in honor of the hockey-playing Herder family, who founded the Evening Telegram in 1879. William J. Herder had seven sons, Arthur, William, Douglas, Augustus, Hubert, Ralph and Jim and all of them had played hockey in St. John's. In fact, at one time the family members formed the nucleus of the Rennies Mill Road team, which challenged and defeated a team of city all-stars in the early 1900s.

Arthur, the eldest, played senior hockey with the St. Andrews team from 1900-02 and went on to study law at Cambridge University. He returned to practice in St. John's and rejoined his old hockey team for two years in 1906-07. Arthur Herder moved to western Canada in 1910, but went overseas with the Royal Newfoundland Regiment in 1914. He died in 1917 from wounds received in France.

William, the second brother, played six years of senior hockey with St. Andrews before joining the Crescents in 1908. He played on three championship teams and was vice-president of the city league from 1929-33. The former president of the Evening Telegram passed away in 1933.

Douglas, as member of the Terra Novas championship team in 1905, was the first member of the Herder family to have his name engraved on the historic Boyle Trophy.

Augustus, the fourth brother, played senior hockey from 1906-21 with the Terra Novas, St. Andrews and the Crescents. He was a member of seven championship teams, which stood as a record up to that time. He came out of retirement to manage the Guards to the Boyle Trophy with an undefeated season in 1923 and was also a director of the Evening Telegram. He died in 1934.

Hubert, the fifth brother, played with the championship Crescents team from 1910-12 before joining the Ontario Agricultural College team for two years. While playing overseas in Scotland, he gained the reputation as being the finest hockey player Newfoundland had ever produced. He was killed at Beaumont Hamel on July 1, 1916.

Ralph, the sixth brother, was a member of the championship Crescents club from 1911-13 before going overseas. He was also wounded during the battle of Beaumont Hamel, but recovered to add two more Boyle Trophies to his collection with the Terra Novas in 1918 and 1919. He passed away in 1953.

The youngest brother, Jim, was a member of the Guards hockey team in the 1930s and was manager of the championship team in 1935 that played against the Corner Brook Royals for the first Herder Memorial Trophy. He died in 1970.

The Avalon Peninsula series became a reality and the Guards defeated Bay Roberts in a two-game total-goal series. At the same time, Corner Brook, Grand Falls and Buchans were playing a series in western Newfoundland, with the Royals holding a healthy lead in their games. Once the Corner Brook squad heard of the proposed series for a provincial championship, they received permission from their western partners to challenge the Guards for the Newfoundland championship.

Permission was sought and obtained from the Herder family to hold the two-game series in St. John's for the Herder Memorial Trophy. The Royals made the long trek from the west coast for their first-ever visit to St. John's. They defeated the Guards to become the first Herder Memorial champions.

St. Bon's of the St. John's league dominated subsequent championship series until 1949, winning 10 of the 12 series played. Bell Island captured its only two Herder trophies in 1941 and 1944. There was no competition during the war years of 1942-43 or during 1991.

The ever-controversial issue of paid players surfaced in the 1950s, when the Buchans Miners imported hockey-playing employees from their operation in Kirkland Lake, Ontario, to compete for the Herder. The strong Buchans teams also added top players from Cape Breton and won four of the next five championships. Grand Falls, tired of playing second fiddle to the Miners, followed suit, bringing in its own paid players and taking six Herders in seven years, including five in a row from 1955-59.

The Conception Bay CeeBees, backed by the Moores family in Harbour Grace, lured brothers George and Alex Faulkner to the bay from Bishop's Falls, and won four championships in the 1960s. The CeeBees became the first Newfoundland team to compete for the prestigious Allan Cup when they played the Moncton Hawks in 1967.

Gander won its first championship in 1969 and, the following year, St. John's reclaimed the Herder for the first time since 1949. The Capitals were a formidable team in the 1970s and even had to divide the team into the Blue Caps and Mike's Shamrocks to keep the senior league alive later in the decade. Interest in the league reached an all-time high during the late 1970s with as many as 11 teams fighting for the coveted trophy during the 1977-78 season.

As Newfoundland teams cast their aspirations to greater heights in the 1980s, the quest for the Allan Cup, signifying senior hockey supremacy in Canada, forced the senior clubs in the province to import high-priced talent to compete for the Newfoundland championship. While the Corner Brook Royals were successful in winning the Allan Cup in 1986, the resulting financial fallout from this venture would cause the demise of the senior league within a few short years.

With budgets reaching as high as $400,000 annually, the senior clubs found themselves in financial trouble and the league finally ceased to function in 1989-90. St. John's and Corner Brook played for the Herder that year, but there was no competition the following season.

The Herder Memorial Trophy was originally put up for competition between local amateur hockey clubs in the province and remained that way for the first 15 years of competition. Because the Herder Memorial Trophy had become part of the culture and history of many towns and cities in the province, a move to have community towns compete for the coveted award was initiated in 1992.

The Newfoundland senior hockey league has come full circle since its opening days, with communities like Badger, La Scie, Flatrock and Southern Shore winning championships in the 1990s. As the Newfoundland and Labrador Hockey Association celebrates its 65th anniversary, the fan interest and competition is as keen as it was in the glory days of senior hockey. The Herder Memorial Trophy lives on in the minds and hearts of senior hockey fans in this province.

Escape the racket.

Have a ball.

Select St. John's and Canada's Far East to host your next competition, championship, or annual general meeting. Participation in your favourite activity and the charm of North America's oldest city – that's a winning combination. Contact the Avalon Convention & Visitors Bureau and talk to our event management experts.

St. John's
&
Canada's Far East

BOX 205, SUITE 201
MURRAY PREMISES, 5 BECK'S COVE
ST. JOHN'S, NF A1C 6H1
PHONE (709) 739-8899 FAX (709) 739-8897
e-mail: info@acvb.nf.net www.CanadasFarEast.com

excellent facilities · competitive hotel rates · incentive programs
bid supports · port facility guides · mailouts to delegates/participants

Marie's
mini mart and deli

congratulates

BREAKWATER

on the

publication

of

Herder
Memorial
TROPHY

———————————

The Early Years

1935-1949

A number of firsts were recorded in Newfoundland hockey history in 1935. The first Avalon Peninsula series was held between the St. John's and Conception Bay champions and the first Herder Memorial Trophy champions were crowned with the initial visit of the Corner Brook Royals to the capital city.

A provisional committee was also struck to oversee the hockey competition in the province. It consisted of chairman Bob Furlong of St. John's, who later became Chief Justice of the Newfoundland Supreme Court, vice-chairman Ron Taaffe of Corner Brook, secretary Arthur Johnson of St. John's, along with committee members Gordon Stirling and Jack Tobin of St. John's and Arthur C. Rendell of Corner Brook.

On the ice, the Guards defeated St. Bon's by a score of 6-4 in a two-game series to win the Boyle Trophy and the city championship, while Bay Roberts ousted Carbonear and Brigus in two games to lay claim to the Conception Bay title.

In the opening game of the Avalon Peninsula series, the Guards got two-goal performances from Hunter Chislett, Harry Drover and Hib Saunders and a single tally from Hector Meadus to defeat Bay Roberts 7-4. Reuben Snow, Bill Russell, Jim Norman and Ron Delaney countered for Bay Roberts. Jim and Bill Norman, Reuben Snow and Ned Russell scored for the Rovers in a 4-3 win in game two, but it was not enough to overcome the Guards' lead in the opening game. Sib Quick, Bob Badcock and Hib Saunders replied for Guards who won the series 10-8.

Heralded as a "new era of sport in Newfoundland", there was great anticipation of exciting hockey as St. John's fans awaited the arrival of the Corner Brook Royals. Ticket sales were brisk and the Prince's Rink was sold out for both games of the series. Herb Coultas refereed the two-game series.

Defenceman Hal Cross scored the only goal 13 minutes into the third period and goaltender Will Fitzpatrick made 41 saves as the Royals edged the Guards 1-0 in the historic first game for the Herder Memorial Trophy. The Royals lost Hal Power to an appendicitis attack following the game and he had to be operated on the next day at St. Clare's Hospital. The Royals were forced to suit up manager Gerry Edens in his place.

The second game of the series turned into a real thriller and the teams were tied 2-2 heading into the third period. Frank Byrne for the Royals and Hector Meadus for the Guards each scored in the first and second periods. Goals by Tony Ledrew and Fred Power in the third frame sent the Royals to their first Herder Trophy.

The members of that historic team included Ron Taaffe as general manager, manager Gerry Edens, goalie Will Fitzpatrick, defencemen Tony Ledrew and Hal Cross, along with forwards Fred Power, Frank Byrne, Frank Marks, Jack Downey and Hal Power.

Three western teams, six from Conception Bay and five in St. John's, entered competition in 1936. Corner Brook again emerged as western champion, travelling to Buchans and defeating the Miners 4-3 and 5-4 after Buchans had eliminated Grand Falls in two straight games, 5-3 and 6-5.

1936

The six-team Conception Bay playoff series was held in St. John's and the final game saw the Bay Roberts Rovers repeat as champions with a 4-1 decision over Bell Island on the strength of goals by Clayton Snow, Bill Russell, Reuben Snow and Bill Norman. Ron Lindsay replied for the Islanders.

In the city, St. Bon's rode the goaltending of Art Hamlyn to a 4-3 victory in the two-game final with the defending champion Guards. St. Bon's won 2-1 in game one and game two was tied 2-2 as Hamlyn stopped 65 shots in the two-game series.

The three-team Herder final was held in St. John's, with Corner Brook edging Bay Roberts 5-4 in overtime in the opening game. Tony Ledrew fired three goals for the Royals who got singles from Hal Power and Frank Byrne in the extra period. Ron Delaney and Reuban Snow each scored twice for the Rovers. St. Bon's received goals from Bob and Charlie Godden, Basil Hutton and Gordon Halley to double Bay Roberts 4-2. Reuben Snow and Ches Sparkes scored in a losing cause. Andy Cahill fired three goals, while Bernie Maher and Charlie Godden had two each, as St. Bon's clobbered Corner Brook 9-1.

The final matched St. Bon's and Corner Brook, with the city team emerging with a 5-2 decision for its first Herder Trophy.

Charlie Godden had two goals, while singles came off the sticks of Ed Brophy, Bob Godden and Andy Cahill. Fred Power and Dave Collins replied for the Royals.

1937

The Buchans Miners emerged as western champions in 1937 as they defeated Corner Brook 7-3 in their series. In St. John's, Cahill scored four goals and collected three assists as St. Bon's defended their championship by defeating the Feildians 11-6. In Conception Bay, Bay Roberts won for the fourth straight season, edging Bell Island 3-2 in the final on Ned Russell's goal in the third overtime period. Harry Roach and Bill Norman also scored for the Rovers, while Bell Island got goals from Phonse Hawco and Bob Petrie.

The three-team Herder final opened in St. John's with St. Bon's blanking Bay Roberts 6-0 in the opening contest. Ed Brophy fired a pair of goals for the winners who got shutout goaltending from Art Hamlyn and single goals from Len Walsh, Jim Vinnicombe, Andy Cahill and Jim Edstrom. Buchans advanced to the final with a 5-3 decision over Bay Roberts as Ralph Colyer fired four goals. Bill Norman had a pair for the Rovers.

Charlie Godden, Jack Vinnicombe, Gerry Hanley and Andy Cahill had single tallies as St. Bon's repeated as Herder champions with a 4-1 victory over Buchans. Bill Traverse had the only goal for the Miners.

1938

As teammates on the St. Bon's team the year before, Art Hamlyn and Andy Cahill led the Bluegolds to a pair of Herder championships. These two players filled the same role in 1938, but with different teams. Andy Cahill still performed his magic on ice for St. Bon's, but Art Hamlyn was recruited by Monsignor Bartlett, the hockey-loving parish priest on Bell Island, to play for the Islanders. Art Hamlyn was instrumental in leading Bell Island to its first Herder final.

St. John's got its first artificial ice surface at the Prince's Rink in November of 1937 when two local junior clubs, the Guards and St. Bon's, played the first game on the new surface. The rink was burned to the ground just four years later, on the night of November 28, 1941.

Art Hamlyn recorded consecutive shutouts as Bell Island ended the four-year Bay Roberts reign in Conception Bay with 2-0 and 3-0 victories. Bob Petrie and Les Coombs scored in the first game, while Ned Penney had a pair and Tom Kent added a single to give Bell Island its first championship.

In the St. John's final, Andy Cahill scored three goals, including two in overtime, as St. Bon's edged the Guards 7-5 in their opening game. Jack Vinnicombe added a pair for St. Bon's, while Sib Quick answered with two for the Guards. Andy Cahill's goal with less than four minutes to go in the game earned St. Bon's another trip to the Herder final with a 2-1 win over the Guards. Ed Berrigan also scored for the winners and Sib Quick replied for the losers.

In the west, Corner Brook opened semi-final play with two straight decisions over Buchans and moved on to Grand Falls for the final. The host team proved to be too much for the Royals and the Papertowners earned their first trip to the Herder final with 4-1 and 3-2 decisions.

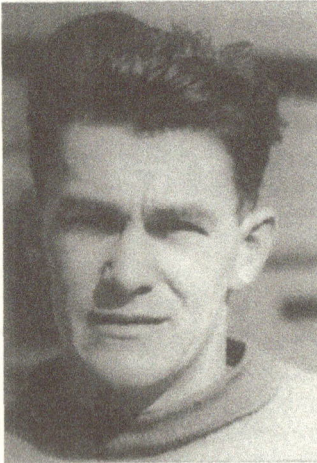

Andy Cahill

Andy Cahill tallied three times, including the winner in overtime, as St. Bon's edged Bell Island 4-3 in the opening game of the final. Ed Berrigan also scored, while Bell Island got two goals from Ned Penney and a single from Bob Petrie. Max Thorne's goal in the third period proved to be the difference as Grand Falls edged Bell Island 3-2 to advance to the Herder final game. Les "Rusty" Irish and Cy Anstey also scored for the Papertowners, while Les Coombs and Tom Kent scored for Bell Island.

Basil Hutton and Ed Berrigan each scored three times, Jack Vinnicombe added two and Andy Cahill notched a single and assisted on five markers as St. Bon's humbled Grand Falls 9-1 in the deciding game for the provincial championship. Ferd Graham also scored for St. Bon's, while Max Power had the lone Grand Falls' goal.

1939

Lloyd Archibald fired three goals to lead Harbour Grace to an 8-2 win over Brigus in the 1939 Conception Bay semi-final. Bill Norman netted a pair of tallies and Ron Snow posted the shutout as Bay Roberts blanked Carbonear 6-0 in the other series. Bay Roberts reclaimed the league title with a 3-1 win over Harbour Grace in overtime as Harry Roach scored twice and Gordon Bradbury added a single. Bill Harris replied for Harbour Grace.

Buchans had a rather easy time in the western playdowns as they defeated Grand Falls by scores of 8-4 and 13-8 and toppled Corner Brook 8-3 in a two-game final series. St. Bon's repeated as city champions with four straight victories in a three-team round robin final with the Feildians and the Guards.

Bell Island and Bay Roberts squared off in a single game to decide the third and final opponent for the round robin Herder championship. Gordon Edwards netted a hat-trick and Tom Kent added a single as Bell Island stopped the Rovers 4-0 behind Art Hamlyn's shutout goaltending.

Goals by Andy Murphy, Gordon Edwards and Les Coombs enabled Bell Island to slip past Buchans 3-2 in the opening game of the final. The losers received markers from former St. Bon's players Bob Godden and Ed Brophy. Les O'Reilly fired five goals, Andy Cahill and Bill Harris each collected five points and Syd Thompson posted the shutout as St. Bon's blasted Buchans 14-0 in the second game.

The final between St. Bon's and Bell Island lived up to its billing as a thriller. The Bluegolds got third-period goals from Bernard Collins and Jack Vinnicombe to blank the Islanders 2-0. Syd Thompson continued his flawless play in the final by making 18 saves for the shutout in a game played before more than 3,000 fans at the Prince's Rink.

1940

The outbreak of the Second World War depleted many teams' rosters in 1940, but St. Bon's, Bell Island and Buchans repeated as winners in their respective leagues. In the west, the Miners stopped Grand Falls 11-8 in their two-game series and earned a trip to the Herder final.

St. Bon's emerged victorious in the city by ousting a stubborn Blue Blades squad in four games in the best-of-five final. Jack Vinnicombe and Bill Harris were the leaders for St. Bon's as each scored six goals in the city championship series.

Ches Sparkes fired two goals as Bay Roberts eliminated Cupids 5-1 in semi-final play in Conception Bay, but the Rovers were no match for Bell Island who claimed the Bay title. The

Islanders got three goals from Gordon Normore and two each from Bob Petrie and Les Coombs on their way to a 12-1 decision.

Goals by Cec Penney and Jack Vinnicombe earned St. Bon's a 2-1 decision over Bell Island in the opening game of the Avalon Peninsula final. Les Coombs replied for the Islanders. Bill Harris notched a pair, while Jack Vinnicombe and Andy Cahill added singles as St. Bon's advanced to the Herder final with a 4-2 decision in game two. Bob Petrie netted both goals in a losing cause.

St. Bon's smothered Buchans 12-l in the opening game of their two-game total-goal series. Les O'Reilly fired five goals, Jack Vinnicombe added four and Andy Cahill had a goal and five assists. Bill Harris and Jim Foley added singles. Ralph Colyer scored for Buchans. With the outcome already decided, Buchans salvaged some respectability in the second game by edging St. Bon's 6-5. Cyril Power led the way with a pair of goals, while Andy Cahill scored twice for St. Bon's who won the series 17 goals to seven.

1941

With more and more players being called into the Armed Forces, several teams requested permission to use Canadian soldiers stationed in Newfoundland for the 1941 Herder playoffs. The requests were denied by the Newfoundland Hockey Association, stating that only Newfoundland players could participate in the playoffs.

Buchans won the western crown by defeating Grand Falls 11-9 in their series, but the Miners would not travel to the city for the Herder final. In St. John's, the Royals pulled off a major upset with a 6-1 decision over St. Bon's to end the Bluegolds' reign on the city title. Edgar Escott and Ted Withers each fired a pair of goals for the new champions who were sponsored by the Royal Stores, a downtown St. John's department store.

The Herder final was reduced to a best-of-three series between Bell Island and the Royals for the Herder Memorial Trophy, with Bell Island opening the series on a 3-2 decision. Gord Edwards, Gord Normore and Hugh Connors scored for Bell Island, while Edgar Escott and Dick Byrne replied for Royals.

Dick Byrne netted three goals, Edgar Escott and Brian Mitchell added two apiece as the Royals knotted the series with a convincing 9-3 triumph. The third game was a thriller, as the Islanders claimed their first Herder Memorial Trophy with a 6-5 decision. Gord Normore paved the way with three goals and singles came from Ned Penney, Bob Petrie and Gord Edwards. Sib Quick scored three times for the Royals who got single tallies from Len Coombs and Dick Byrne.

The player shortage due to enlistments in the Armed Forces limited hockey action to exhibition play in 1942 and 1943. As a result, there were no provincial playoffs held and it wasn't until the spring of 1944 that Newfoundland senior hockey resumed on all fronts.

1944

St. Bon's earned the right to carry the city colours into the 1944 Herder playdowns by defeating the Royals three games to one in the league final. Cyril Power netted four goals as the Bluegolds won the opening game 9-3, while Ed Escott and Ted Withers each scored twice in the Royals' 7-5 decision to tie the series at a game apiece. Bill Harris and Myles Furlong each scored three goals as St. Bon's won game three 9-6, while Bob Withers netted three for Royals. Bill Harris came back with a five-goal performance as St. Bon's won the deciding game 8-6, while Ed Escott scored three and Ted Withers added a pair for the losers.

In the west, Corner Brook stopped Buchans in four straight games to advance to the Herder final. Les O'Reilly tallied three times in a 4-3 win in game one and came back with four goals and three assists in a 9-1 verdict in the second encounter. Don Goodyear scored three goals and Ray Buckle and Les O'Reilly each connected twice as the Royals won game three with an 8-4 decision. Ray Buckle netted six goals and Les O'Reilly added four as the Royals swept the series with a 13-2 victory in the second game at Buchans.

The Avalon series opened on Bell Island with the host team taking a hard-fought 5-4 win over St. Bon's. Gord Normore led the winners with two goals, while Gordon Highmore, Gordon Edwards and Petrie added singles. Jim Kielly, Bill Harris, Cec Penney and Cyril Power connected for the losers. Bill Harris tallied four times, Cyril Power had two and Myles Furlong added another as St. Bon's tied the series with a 7-4 verdict. Gord Edwards had three and Leo Power scored one for Bell Island.

The first controversy in the history of the Newfoundland Senior Hockey League erupted in this series. After the second game, four St. Bon's players had to return to the city for work and a delay was requested for game three. The provincial executive refused the request and the series was awarded to Bell Island, granting the team the the right to advance to the Herder final in Corner Brook. The NAHA had to get permission from the Evening Telegram to hold the final outside St. John's, and this was granted by the paper's publisher, J. M. Herder.

The Islanders won their second straight Herder Memorial Trophy by handing the host Corner Brook team three straight setbacks. Gordon Normore and Ned Penney each scored twice to lead the Islanders to a 7-1 win in the first game, while Bob Petrie connected twice as the Islanders were victorious in the second outing by a 6-5 score. They swept to their second Herder with a 5-1 decision on the strength of two goals by Gord Normore.

1945

The Herder Memorial Trophy became the sole property of St. Bon's for the next five years. The Bluegolds rode the goaltending of Frank Gamberg and John Doyle, along with the offensive prowess of Bill Harris, Cyril Power and Noel Vinnicombe, to five consecutive titles to match their record set between 1936-40.

The 1945 championship series was an all-eastern affair with St. Bon's and the Royals battling for the city title and the right to advance to the Herder final against Bell Island. Playing-coach Bill Harris potted five goals, Cyril Power had three, while Noel Vinnicombe and Cec Penney added two apiece as St. Bon's scored nine goals in the second period to crush the Royals 14-8 in their opening game. Ted Withers scored four times for the losers. Cyril Power added two more goals in a 6-3 decision in the second game to propel St. Bon's to the final.

Bill Power's goal in overtime earned St. Bon's a 4-3 comeback victory in the opening game of the championship series after Bell Island led 3-0 in the first period. Cyril Power connected twice and Hugh Fardy added one for the winners. Brian Murphy had two for the Islanders who got a single marker from Gus Normore. Cyril Power scored three times and set up two goals by Bill Power as the Bluegolds waltzed to a 9-1 win to claim the Herder Trophy. Myles Furlong, Len Walsh, Cec Penney and Noel Vinnicombe also scored for St. Bon's. Gordon Normore had the only Bell Island goal.

1946

St. Bon's had to fight off another stubborn Royals crew to claim the city title in 1946. After Ted Withers' four goals gave the Royals an 8-3 win in the opening game of their series, the Bluegolds roared back with three straight victories to advance to the Herder semi-final. Bill Harris, Myles Furlong, Cyril Power and Bill Power each scored twice in an 8-7 decision in the second game, while Noel Vinnicombe, Cyril Power and Myles Furlong had two apiece as St. Bon's won game three 7-3. Five goals by Bill Power earned the Bluegolds a 9-4 triumph to win the series.

Myles Furlong's pair, combined with singles from Noel Vinnicombe, Bill and Cyril Power, backed the stellar goaltending of Frank Gamberg as St. Bon's opened the Herder semi-final with a 6-0 shutout of Bell Island. Fa Murphy and Bill Power scored three times each as St. Bon's won the series with an 8-6 victory. Cyril Power and Ted Gillies also scored, while Leo Power, Gord Normore and Gerald Rees each connected twice for the Islanders.

Grand Falls swept to the western championship by defeating Corner Brook in straight games of 7-2 and 8-3, but the central team was no match for the powerful St. Bon's squad. Noel Vinnicombe connected four times, Bill Harris added three goals and Fa Murphy and Cyril Power each scored

Bill Harris

twice as St. Bon's won the opening game of the best-of-three Herder final by a lopsided 16-1 score. Noel Vinnicombe was back with another four-goal performance in game two, while Bill Harris and Bill Power backed him up with three each in an 11-4 romp. Fa Murphy had the other goal for St. Bon's, while Leo Delaney netted a pair for Grand Falls. Cec Power and Max Thorne also scored singles for the Grand Falls team.

1947

St. Bon's and Bell Island continued their intense senior hockey rivalry in 1947 in a best-of-three provincial semi-final series that went the limit. Leo Power scored three goals and Bell Island got singles from Brian Murphy, Gord and Gus Normore to edge St. Bon's 6-5 in the opening game. Bill Harris scored twice in a losing cause. Bill Power scored twice and Ted Withers added a single as St. Bon's evened the series with a 3-1 decision. The shutout goaltending of Frank Gamberg and two goals from Ted Withers decided the series outcome with St. Bon's blanking Bell Island 5-0 in the deciding game.

Grand Falls opened the western playoffs by stopping Bishop's Falls 18-10 in their two-game series. The Grand Falls club won the first game 10-2 and the teams tied 8-8 in the second contest. A late third-period goal by Les Irish earned Grand Falls a 10-9 two-game series win over Corner Brook and a berth in the Herder final. Corner Brook won the opening game of the series 6-4, but Grand Falls rebounded with a 6-3 victory in the second game.

The Herder final was held in Gander for the first time and it was an outstanding four-goal performance from Noel Vinnicombe that decided the outcome of the series in game one as St. Bon's doubled Grand Falls 8-4. The teams battled to a 4-4 tie in the second game, but the four-goal cushion from the first game carried the Bluegolds to another Herder Memorial Trophy. Noel Vinnicombe, Fa Murphy, Ted Withers and Cyril Power connected for St. Bon's, while the Grand Falls scorers were Cy Anstey (with two), Les Irish and Allan Dwyer.

1948

The 1948 battle for the Herder Trophy opened with four teams competing in the eastern playoffs and five more in the west. In western playoff action, Buchans eliminated Gander and Bishop's Falls to advance to the western semi-final against Grand Falls. Brian Mitchell netted a pair of goals as the Miners doubled Grand Falls 4-2 in the opening game of their series, while Al Mullins scored twice as Buchans completed the sweep with a 6-2 victory to advance to the final against the Corner Brook Royals. The Miners continued their dominance in the playoffs by sweeping past the Royals with scores of 9-5 and 8-3.

In the eastern playdowns, Reuben Snow notched a pair of goals as Bay Roberts slipped past Harbour Grace 5-4 to open the Conception Bay series. Reuben Snow added another goal in the second game, won by the Rovers 3-2. Ted Withers netted a hat-trick and John Doyle posted the shutout as St. Bon's blanked Bell Island 5-0 in the first game of their series. Ted

Withers, Noel Vinnicombe, Jack Reardigan and Cyril Power all scored as the Bluegolds doubled the Miners 4-2 in the second game. Riv Ford and Leo Power replied for the Islanders.

St. Bon's dominated the Herder semi-final against Bay Roberts, winning 12-3 and 10-0. Fa Murphy pulled the trigger on three goals in the first game, while Jack Reardigan, Ted Withers and Noel Vinnicombe added two apiece. Ted Withers connected four times in the second contest, while Cyril Power added three goals and Noel Vinnicombe scored twice. Frank Gamberg posted the shutout.

St. Bon's travelled to Grand Falls for the best-of-three Herder final against a strong Buchans team. The Bluegolds won both games, adding their ninth Herder Trophy to their collection. Cyril Power netted two goals and Bill Corbett and Myles Furlong each scored singles as St. Bon's won the opening game 4-2. Brian Mitchell and George Pike replied for Buchans. Cyril Power's second goal of the game with two seconds remaining earned St. Bon's a 2-1 decision in the title contest. Bob Piercey scored for Buchans.

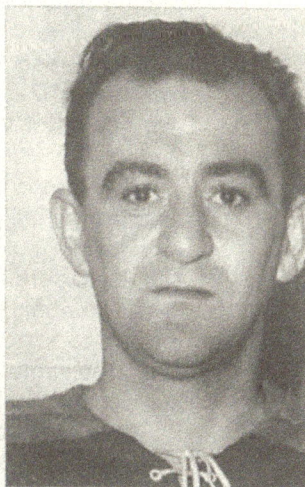

Noel Vinnicombe

1949

St. Bon's showed their rivals no mercy as the 1949 Herder Trophy playoffs opened. The Bluegolds had four goals from Ted Withers, three from Ted Gillies and two apiece from Cyril Power, Hugh Fardy and Noel Vinnicombe to outscore Bell Island 14-7. Leo Rees and Bill Power each scored three times for the losers. Ted Withers added four more goals in the second game as St. Bon's trounced the Islanders 16-5. Cyril Power and Bill Corbett each added three goals and Damien Ryan netted a pair. Riv Ford and Leo Rees each scored twice for Bell Island.

In the opening round in the west, Ron Mullins and Bill Scott, a St. John's native given a job and paid to play hockey in the mining town, each scored twice as Buchans edged past Grand Falls 6-4. The Miners had hoped to have new players from Ontario in their lineup that season, but were forced to use local players when the imports did not arrive in Newfoundland in time for the player registration deadline. Grand Falls evened the series with a 7-4 decision in game two as Les Irish and Ed Walsh each scored twice. Ed Walsh added two more, while Charlie Shallow, Wats Goobie and Roger Howse also scored as Grand Falls upset Buchans 5-2 in the deciding game. Ed Walsh continued his torrid scoring pace with a pair of goals in each game as Grand Falls eliminated Gander in two straight games by scores of 7-3 and 8-2. Don Dean and Eric Lannon also had two-goal efforts for Grand Falls. Al Folkes notched a pair for Gander.

Grand Falls opened the western final in Corner Brook, but the Royals were poor hosts as they drubbed the visiting Grand Falls team 10-3 behind the two-goal efforts of Bob Doucette and Roy Oxford. There was a full house in attendance in Corner Brook awaiting the start of the second game, but Grand Falls refused to start the contest, complaining of poor ice conditions. The game was awarded to the Royals who entertained St. Bon's in the final.

Noel Vinnicombe netted four goals, Ted Withers added three and Cyril Power notched a pair as St. Bon's opened their first-ever visit to Corner Brook with a 13-3 victory. Jack Reardigan, Hugh Fardy, Damien Ryan and Myles Furlong added singles. Roy Oxford, Tony Dwyer and Gerry Myrden replied for the Royals. Noel Vinnicombe and Ted Withers scored twice apiece and singles came from Jack Reardigan, Fa Murphy, Damien Ryan and Cyril Power as the Bluegolds captured their tenth and final Herder with an 8-3 decision to sweep the series. Tony Dwyer, Roy Oxford and Bob Doucette had the Corner Brook goals.

While the early years of provincial senior hockey focused on the use of local players for the senior championship, teams throughout the province felt they would need to import better players if they were to be competitive with St. Bon's and wrest the Herder Memorial Trophy from the capital city. Player movement began in earnest after the Bluegolds' 1949 triumph and local players in several communities were often left on the sidelines as the battle for the provincial senior hockey championship heated up.

Part of the Team

At The Co-operators,
community
involvement
is an important
part of our
core values.

We know that team work is the key
to success, that's why we're proud
to sponsor the books of the
Our Sports Heritage collection.

the co-operators
A Better Place For You™

Home   Auto   Life   RRSPs
Farm   Business   Group

Accident and Injury Lawyers
with a Proven Track Record

WILLIAMS ♦ ROEBOTHAN
McKay ♦ MARSHALL
BARRISTERS, SOLICITORS & NOTARIES

Proud Supporter of the
OUR SPORTS HERITAGE
collection.

(709) 753-5805
Toll Free 1-800-563-5563(24-Hour Service)

2

SOS Send Players Please

The arrival of hockey-playing employees at the Buchans Mining Company opened a new chapter in Newfoundland senior hockey history. The introduction of imports and paid professional coaches and players into the local amateur hockey ranks has been viewed in positive and negative lights for the past 50 years. But there can be no denying the immediate impact these players had on the Buchans Miners team in the early 1950s. Hockey was more than a game to the people of Buchans. The Buchans Social and Athletic Club was formed to co-ordinate activities for the community that were centred around the rink during the cold winter days and nights in the central Newfoundland town. General skating and hockey provided the residents with plenty of social activity. The company even provided extra train cars so fans could accompany the Miners to games in Grand Falls, Corner Brook and Gander.

Upset because his team was beaten by St. Bon's in the Herder final, Buchans mine manager Mr. George Thomas put in a call to the sister mining operation in Kirkland Lake, Ontario, to send hockey players to Buchans. The move paid off with the Miners capturing the Herder four times in the next five years. Grand Falls quickly followed, recruiting and paying players in an attempt to beat their rivals. The precedent was set and other teams began to bring in mainland players. The Conception Bay CeeBees were formed in the same manner when former Newfoundland Premier Frank Moores combined the best players from the Bishop's Falls, Grand Falls and Bell Island teams in an effort to capture the elusive Herder Memorial Trophy.

1950

St. Bon's continued to dominate the hockey picture in the east with their repeat as Avalon Peninsula champions in 1950 with two convincing victories over Bell Island. A three-goal performance by Bill Corbett and two-goal efforts by Bob Furlong, Cyril Power and Jack Ryan paced the Bluegolds to a 12-2 decision in the first game. Cyril Power, Noel Vinnicombe, Bill Corbett and Hugh Fardy each connected twice as St. Bon's won the second encounter 10-3. Bell Island had earned the Conception Bay championship when Brigus defaulted the scheduled third game of their series with the teams tied at a game apiece.

Grand Falls opened the western playoffs as they downed Gander by scores of 8-5 and 16-5. Gerald "Markie" Andrews led Grand Falls with five goals and four assists in the series, while Al Folkes, Gerry Woods and Dave Green each chipped in with three goals. As strong as Grand Falls felt it was, the Papertowners were no match for the powerful Buchans squad bolstered by the addition of Frank Bowman, Scottie McPhail and Tom Barrett from Cape Breton. The Miners drubbed Grand Falls by scores of 17-2 and 9-2 in the semi-final with Barrett and Art "Copper" Laite each scoring five times and import Ken Joy adding three goals and six assists. The Miners ran up ever bigger scores when they beat Corner Brook 20-5 and 20-1. Tom Barrett netted eight goals in the opening game, while Herb Pike added three and Jim Hornell chipped in with a pair. Tom Barrett scored four times in the second encounter and Jim Hornell and Copper Laite followed with three apiece.

The stage was set in Grand Falls for the Herder final between the five-time defending champions from St. Bon's and the upstart Buchans Miners. Extra seats had to be constructed in the Grand Falls Arena to bring the seating capacity to 4,000, the most to ever watch a hockey game in central Newfoundland.

A five-goal third-period outburst, combined with two-goal performances from Copper Laite, Jim Hornell and Tom Barrett, paced the Miners to a 9-3 decision in the opening game. Noel Vinnicombe notched two goals for St. Bon's and Ted Gillies added a single. The Miners completed the sweep for their first Herder Trophy with an 8-2 verdict in the second game. Tom Barrett led the way with five goals, and singles came from Scottie McPhail, Red Croteau and George Pike. Noel Vinnicombe and Damien Ryan scored for the losers.

Copper Laite was described as the best player ever to come out of Buchans and went on to play major junior hockey and senior hockey in Quebec City with the Citadels and Aces. In fact, one of his teammates with the senior Aces was former Montreal Canadiens star Jean Beliveau.

1951

The 1951 season was a carbon copy of the previous year. The powerful Buchans squad demolished everything in its path in the western playoffs. They opened the playoffs by stopping Grand Falls 11-2 and 5-1 as Allie Carver, Bernie "Bessie" MacDonald and Jim Hornell each scored three goals in the series. Doug Foote was outstanding in the Grand Falls goal as Buchans fired 132 shots his way, including 73 in the first game. The Miners handed Gander 14-0 and 13-3 setbacks and pummeled Corner Brook on the west coast by scores of 29-1 and 25-1. Bessie MacDonald, who played with the Moncton Hawks and the Sydney Millionaires prior to coming to Newfoundland, had 16 goals and two assists against Corner Brook, while Jim Hornell, from Kirkland Lake, added four goals and eight helpers for 12 points. Newcomer Willie Robertson added six goals, while Allie Carver and George Pike had five goals each.

St. Bon's had a relatively easy time in the eastern playoffs with two straight victories over Bell Island. Ted Gillies, Hugh Fardy and Noel Vinnicombe each scored three goals in a 14-5 victory as Hubert Power tallied twice for Bell Island. Ted Gillies netted three goals and Jim McNamara, Ed Manning and Hugh Fardy added two each as St. Bon's moved to the Herder final with a 10-8 decision. Gord Normore led the Bell Island squad with three markers and Bill Power and Leo Rees added two each.

Two more capacity crowds filled the Grand Falls Stadium as the Miners and the Bluegolds faced off again for the Herder Memorial Trophy. Three-goal outbursts in the first and third periods enabled Buchans to win the opening game 6-2 as Allie Carver led the way with two goals. Noel Vinnicombe and Ed Manning replied in a losing cause. Allie Carver was back in game two with a four-goal effort and the Miners tallied three times in the first period to stop St. Bon's 6-2 for its second Herder championship. Ted Gillies netted both goals in a losing cause. Allie Carver and St. Bon's goaltender John Doyle were selected as the top players in the series. Allie Carver collected six goals and two assists, while John Doyle was outstanding in goal as Buchans fired 85 shots at the agile netminder in the two games.

1952

Buchans continued to have a field day in the western playoffs in 1952. Willie Robertson scored 12 goals in a two-game rout of Grand Falls as the Miners won 15-2 and 13-2. The Miners then toppled Gander 8-1 and 9-2. As bad as the scores were the two previous years against Corner Brook, they got worse this time with Buchans humiliating the Royals 27-3 and 28-3 in the two-game series. The Miners' top line of Allie Carver, Willie Robertson and Al Mullins scored 33 of the goals. The Miners were so dominant that Allie Carver and Willie Robertson each tallied twice while the Miners were serving the game's only minor penalty. Biff Hull and Gaetan Plasse each had three goals for the Royals.

St. Bon's opened defence of the Avalon Peninsula championship with a two-game sweep of Brigus at Bell Island. Ted Gillies notched four goals, while Jack Reardigan, Jack Ryan, Cyril Power and Jim McNamara had two apiece in a 14-5 decision. Howard Roberts had two goals for the losers. Cyril Power collected five goals and Noel Sparrow added three as St. Bon's trounced the Bruins 24-3 in the second game with an 11-goal uprising in the first period.

Ted Gillies and Cyril Power collected hat-tricks as St. Bon's slipped past Bell Island 8-5 to open the eastern final. Jack Reardigan and Hugh Fardy added single tallies. Gerald Connors had two for Bell Island who got singles from Gerry MacDonald, Kit Rees and Bill Power. The Bluegolds claimed the championship with another 8-5 victory in game two. Ted Gillies, Bill Corbett and Jack Ryan each scored twice, while Hugh Fardy and Cyril Power chipped in with singles. Bill Stone and Hubert Power scored two goals apiece for Bell Island and Gerald Connors had one.

Goals by Bill Scott, Bob McKinley, Bill Kelly, Herb Pike, Ray Morrison, Willie Robertson and Allie Carver earned Buchans a 7-1 win in the opening game of the Herder final. Ed Manning replied for St. Bon's. Willie Robertson netted three tallies and Bill Scott added a pair from his defence slot as Buchans won its third straight

Bill Scott

Herder with a 5-2 victory. Cyril Power and Jack Reardigan answered for St. Bon's. The losers got another outstanding goaltending performance from John Doyle who made 81 saves in the series as Buchans outshot St. Bon's 93-48.

The Newfoundland Hockey Association elected Ross Moore of Grand Falls as its new president in 1952 and Walter Clarke of Grand Falls took over the reins as secretary-treasurer. In addition, the association drew up a schedule for the following year that would streamline the Herder Memorial Trophy playoffs.

1953

The 1953 Herder playoffs started out as scheduled with the Grand Falls All-Stars posting a pair of lopsided shutout victories over Gander. Import Ray Marshall and George Faulkner, a rookie out of Bishop's Falls, each scored two goals as Grand Falls won the opening game 13-0. Al Folkes registered a hat-trick in the second game, a 9-0 whitewash. Goaltender Doug Foote recorded both shutouts.

The St. John's winner was supposed to travel to Grand Falls for the next round, but the city league decided to withdraw from provincial competition because mild weather on the east coast resulted in poor ice-making conditions. As a result, the league felt there were not enough games played that year for the city teams to be competitive in the Herder playoffs. Bell Island and the Conception Bay league also decided not to compete. To make matters worse, the Corner Brook Royals withdrew just prior to their scheduled series with the Buchans Miners, leaving only Buchans and Grand Falls to battle it out for the Herder Trophy.

This season marked the arrival of Hugh "Red" Wadden and Frank Walker to Buchans. The two Cape Breton hockey players were signed to one-year deals with the club, but both have remained in the mining town ever since and have become household names in provincial senior hockey circles. Hugh Wadden played right up until his retirement in the late 1960s, while an eye injury cut Frank Walker's career short a few years prior.

With 6,200 fans attending the two games in Grand Falls, the fans didn't go home disappointed as Grand Falls under the coaching of Wes Trainor, won its first Herder Memorial Trophy. The club got a two-goal performance from Ray Marshall to open the series with an electrifying 6-4 decision over the

Miners. George Faulkner, playing with two broken fingers and a special leather glove made at Joe Byrne's sport shop, added a goal and two assists, while Clar Goulding, Joe Byrne and Fred Sanger added singles. Pat Kennedy netted two goals for Buchans and singles were added by Willie Robertson and Allie Carver. The deciding game resulted in a 4-1 victory for Grand Falls. Ray Marshall, Dave Green, Joe Byrne and George Faulkner scored, while Lubin Bisson had the only goal for Buchans who had fallen behind 3-0 after the first period. Doug Foote was rewarded for his fine play in the series and was named the most valuable player.

The teams from the east coast carried the issue of paid players to a hot and heavy annual meeting of the provincial association where Ralph Colyer of Buchans was elected president to succeed Moore. The western teams decided to maintain the import players in an attempt to improve hockey in their respective communities and compete for the Herder. Teams opting to use only local players formed the Newfoundland senior "B" division. The Evening Telegram Trophy was donated for this playoff.

1954

The controversy over the paid player issue continued to rage throughout the 1953-54 hockey season. St. John's decided it would not enter provincial play against professional hockey players, leaving only Buchans and Grand Falls to compete for the Herder Trophy. The new section "B" Evening Telegram series drew interest from Gander, Grand Falls and Bell Island.

Gander advanced to the final in section "B" by sweeping two games from the Grand Falls Bees. Grand Falls was short-handed for the second game when coach Wes Trainor sent five players home because they were 15 minutes late arriving back at their hotel after game one. Grand Falls rugged defenceman Walt Davis displayed his toughness in the opening game against Gander. He was clipped by an errant high stick from Taylor Gordon and was taken to hospital in Gander. "I remember waiting a

Wes Trainor

long time for someone to look at me," he recalled. "The game was on the radio in the next room. When we fell behind after the second period, I called a taxi and rushed back to play the third period. It was only after the game that I returned to hospital and received seven stitches to close the cut in my head."

Bell Island opened the "B" final with a 3-2 decision over Gander on goals from George Connors, Ed Ford and Dean Reeves. Fa Murphy tallied both goals for Gander. Taylor Gordon, who later went on to be one of Canada's top boxing coaches, Bob Linehan, Joe McGuire and John Murphy scored singles as Gander evened the series with a 4-2 win in the second game. Riv Ford and Hap McDonald replied for Bell Island. Hap McDonald netted two goals for Bell Island in the deciding game as the Miners won the championship with a 6-5 victory. Gord Skanes, Ed Ford, Hubert Power and Gerald Connors added singles. Bob Linehan led Gander with a pair, and singles went to Taylor Gordon and John Murphy. Gerald Connors, a 27-year-old defenceman with the Islanders, was named the top player for his team after scoring the winning goal in the third game, while Bob Linehan was best for Gander with three goals and three assists in the series.

Grand Falls opened defence of the Herder Memorial Trophy with an 8-6 win in the opening game against Buchans. Jim McDonald led the winners with three goals and two assists, while singles came from Clar Goulding, Ed Danyluk, Markie Andrews, Buck Hannaford and Duck MacLean. Import Danny McNeill paced the Miners with two goals and two assists. Hugh Wadden added a pair, and singles came from imports Jim Hornell and Gerry Casey.

Dan McNeill came back with three goals in the second game to lead Buchans to an 8-2 triumph. Hugh Wadden added four points for the winners, while an 18-year-old rookie import, speedster Clobie Collins, notched his first Newfoundland senior hockey league playoff goal for Grand Falls.

Gerry Casey's goal with 1:47 left on the clock gave the Miners a 4-3 victory and the championship in the third game. Dan McNeill led the Miners with two goals and

Clobie Collins

Al Mullins netted the other. Jim McDonald, Andrews and Eric Bartlett replied for Grand Falls. Buchans goaltender Sham McInnis and Grand Falls forward Jim McDonald were named top players in the series. Dan McNeill, with seven goals and three assists, walked off with the Sherwood Trophy for top scorer in the finals.

1955

The St. John's Hockey League maintained its position of not competing for the Herder in 1955 because teams were still using paid players. Instead, the league decided to enter an all-star team in the senior "B" eastern playoffs against Bell Island. The defending champion Islanders proved to be too powerful for the city contingent and took both games of the best-of-three series by 5-4 and 12-9 scores. Interest in the series attracted fans in record numbers as 5,795 spectators paid to view the second game at St. John's Memorial Stadium.

George Connors netted two goals for Bell Island in the opening game singles from Joe Byrne, Gord Skanes and Bill Power. Jack Ryan scored twice for the Caps, with singles coming from Cyril Power and Don Smith for the Caps. Unfortunately, the game on Bell Island was marked with one ugly incident when Bell Island defenceman Tom Cobb cracked St. John's forward Jack Reardigan over the head with his stick. The blow sent Reardigan to hospital for an overnight stay.

Hubert Power, Dean Reeve and Bill Power each connected for two goals to pace Bell Island in the second game. Singles came off the sticks of Joe Byrne, Gerald Connors, Ed Ford, Hap MacDonald, George Connors and Cyril Power. Jack Ryan tallied four times for the city squad and Don Smith added a pair. Singles came from Noel Sparrow, Bill Corbett and Ted Gillies.

Grand Falls and Gander squared off in the western series and the Grand Falls Bees skated to 7-4 and 7-3 decisions to advance to the final. Cec Power paced the opening win with three goals and Eric Bartlett netted a pair. Seth Lindhal and John French chipped in with singles. Jack MacArthur paced Gander with two goals and Bill Ireland and Joe McGuire had one apiece. Cec Power connected three times in game two, while singles came from Roy Davis, Jim Temple and Tom Granter. Joe McGuire, John Murphy and Jack MacArthur replied in a losing cause.

The final between Bell Island and Grand Falls was played at Memorial Stadium in St. John's and 5,000 fans witnessed a strong Grand Falls squad hammer Bell Island 11-4 in the first game of the best-of-three series for the Evening Telegram Trophy. Seth Lindhal led the winners with three goals and three assists, while Eric Bartlett and Clar Dwyer each netted a brace. John French had a goal and four assists, while single tallies came from Lindy Faulkner, Roy Byrne and Cec Power. Bill Power had two for the Islanders who also enjoyed singles from Hap MacDonald and Gordie Butler.

"That was our first game in Memorial Stadium and I remember how hot it was on the ice," Walt Davis recalled. "I also remember the organist playing slow music when we had the puck and really turning up the pace when Bell Island had it. It almost put us to sleep."

More than 5,000 fans were on hand to see a five-goal performance from George Connors lift Bell Island to a 7-3 verdict to tie the series. Gordie Butler and Leo Cole also scored for the winners. Neil Knight had two for Grand Falls and Tom Granter added a single.

The third and deciding game attracted a record crowd of over 6,000 fans as Bell Island repeated as senior "B" champions with a 5-4 win over Grand Falls in overtime. George Connors' third goal of the game after 33 seconds of extra play earned him most valuable player honours in the series and the title for the Islanders. Dean Reeve and Cyril Power also scored for the winners, while Gerry Woods led Grand Falls with two markers. Jim Temple and Roy Byrne chipped in with singles.

Competition for the Herder Memorial Trophy in 1955 was limited to teams from Grand Falls and Buchans and the Grand Falls Andcos beginning their five-year reign as champions. The Andcos defeated the Miners three games to one in a best-of-five series. Three goals from Wats Goobie and a pair from rookie Alex Faulkner led Grand Falls to an 8-4 victory in the opening game. George Howse, John MacKenzie and Buck Hannaford scored singles. Al Mullins and Hugh Wadden scored twice each for the Miners. John MacKenzie, Clobie Collins and Vic Grignon had a goal apiece as Grand Falls moved into the driver's seat in the series with a 3-2 win in game two. Al Mullins and Dan McNeill replied for the losers.

Roy Mullins, Jim Hornell and Al Mullins each had a goal as Buchans stayed alive in the series with a thrilling 3-2 win in the third encounter. Clobie Collins and Clar Goulding had goals in a losing cause. The Andcos put the finishing touches on a successful series by trouncing the injury-riddled Miners 8-1 in the fourth and deciding game. Buck Hannaford, Alex Faulkner and Vic Grignon each connected twice for Grand Falls, while playing-coach Wes Trainor and John MacKenzie chipped in with singles. Tom Loder answered for Buchans.

1956

The 1956 eastern senior "B" final proved to be a real homer series as Bell Island and St. John's squared off once again. Four goals by Hal Sheppard and three each from Bill Power and Cyril Power led the Islanders to a convincing 15-5 decision in the opening game. George Phillips was the top city shooter with a pair of goals. Goalie Irv Walsh stopped 42 shots and Cy Hoskins scored twice as St. John's took an 8-1 victory at Memorial Stadium. The deciding game was played on Bell Island and the home team thrashed the Capitals 15-1 with Bill Power tallying four times and Ed Ford and Reeve adding three apiece. Cyril Power chipped in with a pair.

The Islanders, coached by Neil Amadio, received outstanding goaltending from Joe Penney and goals from George Connors, Mike Norcott, Gordie Butler and Hubert Power to stop Grand Falls 4-1 in the opening game of the provincial final. Hal

Sheppard netted three goals to pace the Islanders to another championship with a hard-fought 5-4 decision in the second game. Gordie Butler and George Connors added singles for the Islanders. Grand Falls had two goals from Neil Knight and one apiece from Cec Power and Jim Temple.

St. John's decided to re-enter competition for the Herder Memorial Trophy in 1956 and elected to send its first-place team, St. Bon's, into battle in the provincial semi-final against the Buchans Miners. Ted Gillies' goal in overtime earned the Bluegolds a 7-6 win in the opening game. Ted Gillies and Ed Manning each had three markers for the winners and Hugh Fardy scored once. Cy Doucette netted three tallies for Buchans, while Hugh Wadden, Jack Cooper and Frank

Frank Walker

Walker had one each. Buchans got goals from seven different players to tie the series with a 7-2 decision. They advanced to the provincial final by stopping St. Bon's 8-1 in the deciding game with strong two-goal performances from Frank Walker and Hugh Wadden.

The Miners proved to be no match for Grand Falls in the Herder final. Led by playoff most valuable player and top scorer, Alex Faulkner, the Andcos took three games to claim their second consecutive title.

Clobie Collins scored three times, while Alex Faulkner and John MacKenzie sniped a pair as Grand Falls opened the series with a 10-4 decision. Dan McNeill scored twice in a losing cause. John MacKenzie and Buck Hannaford each scored a pair in the Grand Falls 8-3 victory in the second game. Al Folkes had two goals and Alex Faulkner added a goal and two assists, giving him 10 points for the series, as Grand Falls completed the sweep of the Miners with a resounding 10-0 triumph in the third contest.

1957

For only the third time since its inception in 1935, there was no competition for the Herder Memorial Trophy in 1957. The popularity of the senior "B" championships continued to draw teams from all over the island, but nobody wanted to compete with Grand Falls, an "A" club sprinkled with imports, mainly from the Nova Scotia senior league. When Bell Island, senior "B" champions for three years running, decided not to enter the Herder playoffs, the Newfoundland Amateur Hockey Association awarded the Herder to Grand Falls without a game ever being played.

"I wasn't quite sure what happened that year," claimed Alex Faulkner when asked about the incident. "I remember getting the Herder Trophy, but I can't remember ever playing a game for it." He blamed Bell Island coach Joe Byrne for trying to manipulate the team rosters so Bell Island would have a stronger "B" team than Grand Falls for the playoffs. "When that trick didn't work, they knew they couldn't beat us in either division and they dropped out," he said.

The senior "B" playoffs opened in Corner Brook where the Royals swept two straight games from the Gander Flyers. Gord Staples fired a pair of goals to lead the Royals to a 5-3 decision in game one and Ed O'Quinn, Ron Martin and Doug Hillis added singles. Jim Wells had two for Gander and Bill Ireland chipped in with one. Goals by Ed Roche, George Aucoin and Gord Staples lifted the Royals to a 3-1 victory and the series win. John Murphy replied in a losing cause.

In "B" semi-final action, Grand Falls got two-goal performances from brothers Alex and Lindy Faulkner, Clobie Collins, Vic Grignon and Jim Temple to smother Corner Brook 11-2. The Bees won the second game 7-3 as Buck Hannaford notched a pair of goals. Corner Brook goaltender Bert Brake was the star of that game, making 57 saves.

In the eastern playoffs, Bell Island and St. John's hooked up again and the Islanders maintained their superiority over the Capitals. George Connors clicked for a hat-trick as Bell Island stopped the Capitals 7-3 in one game, while a late third-period goal by Bill Norcott earned Bell Island a trip to the final with a 4-3 win over St. John's.

The 1957 championship final for the Evening Telegram Trophy goes on record as the longest series ever played in Newfoundland. The best-of-seven final opened in Grand Falls in March with the host team winning the first game 5-3 as Clobie Collins scored three goals and Alex Faulkner added three assists. Vic Grignon and Jim Temple chipped in with singles. Mike Norcott led the Islanders with two goals and Hubert Power netted one.

Alex Faulkner

In the second game, Alex Faulkner displayed the brilliance that would later land him in the National Hockey League. The diminutive centreman led Grand Falls with six goals, including three within a record-setting 19 seconds in the third period, as his mates beat the Islanders 15-5. Buck Hannaford chipped in with three markers and Cec Thomas netted a pair. Hal Sheppard was the lone bright spot for the losers with a pair of tallies.

Vince Rossiter was elected president of the provincial association during the annual meeting in St. John's in the spring of 1957 and his first major task was to try and get the senior "B" championships completed. Grand Falls travelled to Bell Island to complete the series the following weekend,

40

but ice conditions in Conception Bay halted the ferry traffic for several days. Bad weather conditions prevailed for the next three weeks and it wasn't until April 16 that the Grand Falls club was able to reach Bell Island.

When play resumed, Grand Falls won the third game by a 14-7 count as Clobie Collins, perhaps the fastest skater ever to play senior hockey in Newfoundland, scored three times. The winners had two-goal performances from Alex Faulkner, Clar Goulding, Jim Temple and Vic Grignon. Cyril Power and Mike Norcott each had two for the Islanders. Alex Faulkner, Clobie Collins and Buck Hannaford each scored three times and Jim Temple added a pair as Grand Falls became the first team to win the senior "A" and "B" championships in the same season with a 14-3 win over Bell Island to sweep the series 4-0.

1958

The Grand Falls Bees continued their dominance of the senior "B" league in 1958 as they opened defence of their title with three convincing victories over Corner Brook in the western semi-final. Lindy Faulkner and Vic Grignon each fired three goals in an 11-2 romp, while Clar Goulding and Terry Jesseau each notched a hat-trick in a 15-2 decision. Clobie Collins tallied four times, while Terry Jesseau and Vic Grignon added three apiece as the Bees smothered the west coast squad 15-2.

Gander opened the other western semi-final with a 7-3 victory over Buchans on the strength of three goals by Bill Ireland and two by Frank Pacquette. But the Miners had two-goal efforts from Roy Mullins and Hugh Wadden to nip the Flyers 7-6 to even the series. Third-period goals by John Murphy and Ed Doheny propelled Gander to a 5-3 win in game three and they wrapped up the series with a 9-5 decision as Dave Gilhen scored three times.

The speedy Grand Falls forwards, led by Clobie Collins, Alex Faulkner and Vic Grignon, hammered out a pair of decisive victories over the visiting Flyers, winning 11-3 and 13-1. They went on to wrap up a berth in the provincial final by stopping the Flyers 7-5 in Gander as Clobie Collins contributed another four-goal game. Frank Pacquette was tops for Gander with three goals.

St. John's and Bell Island met for the fourth straight year in the eastern final, but this time the Capitals finally prevailed. Paced by the shutout goaltending of Merv Greene and two goals from Noel Sparrow, the Caps opened the series with a 3-0 victory. However, Nick Kennedy notched a pair of goals to lead Bell Island to a 6-2 decision that tied the series. Nick Kennedy's goal gave Bell Island a 1-0 lead for two periods in game three, but third-period markers by Ted Gillies and Bern Goobie earned the Capitals a 2-1 win and the series lead. Hugh Fardy scored three times and Lloyd Kelly added a pair as St. John's won the deciding contest 7-4 despite a two-goal effort from George Connors for the losers.

Grand Falls hosted St. John's to open the "B" final and took the first two games from the Capitals by scores of 6-4 and 8-1. Buck Hannaford and Alex Faulkner scored two goals each in the first game, while Cyril Ivany had two for the losers. Buck Hannaford, Alex Faulkner and Jim Temple were two-goal marksmen in the second contest.

St. John's got back in the series when it shifted to Memorial Stadium with a 4-3 decision as Ted Gillies fired three goals, but Grand Falls regained a two-game lead with a 7-5 victory as Heber Rideout and Buck Hannaford scored twice apiece. Mike Woodford netted two goals for the Capitals. Grand Falls clinched the championship with a 5-1 win as Alex Faulkner scored two goals.

The Bees became the first Newfoundland senior hockey team to play for the Atlantic Provinces senior "B" title when they hosted the Nova Scotia champions from Windsor in April. Despite two-goal performances from Lindy Faulkner and Clobie Collins, the Bees dropped a 13-5 decision in the opening game and were eliminated via an 8-2 score in the second game.

Imported playing-coaches highlighted the battle for the Herder Memorial Trophy in 1958 as Grand Falls and Corner Brook met in a best-of-seven series. The Grand Falls lineup included Orin Carver, Sherm White and Tom Blackmore, while the Royals were led by Jack Lane and Joe Iannarelli. Orin Carver was the brother of Allie Carver who toiled for the Buchans Miners earlier in the decade.

It took two overtime periods to settle the opening game. In the end, Grand Falls won 11-10 with Orin Carver and Ralph Cook scoring three times apiece. Jack Lane led the Royals with four goals and Rod Kennedy chipped in with three. Orin Carver notched three more in the second game as Grand Falls stopped the Royals 8-3. Alfie Hiscock, who had two goals in game one, chipped in with three markers and Tom Blackmore also had a pair. Joe Iannarelli led the Royals with two goals.

Cyril Oldford and Jack Lane each netted two goals as Corner Brook surprised the Andcos in game three at Humber Gardens 7-3. Orin Carver was back with two more goals to lead Grand Falls to a 4-1 triumph in game four. Grand Falls clinched another Herder in the fifth game with a 9-3 victory as Orin Carver, Alfie Hiscock and Roger Dean each scored twice. Orin Carver, who later coached at Memorial University and played senior hockey in St. John's, made quite an impression in the final series as he scored 10 goals and collected eight assists in the five games.

Orin Carver

1959

The Conception Bay CeeBees arrived on the provincial hockey scene in 1959. George Faulkner had just returned from a four-year stint in Quebec and was hired to coach the team. He lured his brother, Alex, away from Grand Falls to become the playing-coach of the Harbour Grace entry in the Conception Bay North League. Defenceman Jim Kennedy, also from Bishop's Falls, joined the initial crew of players. The CeeBees also signed goalie Murray Matheson from Nova Scotia.

"We only had three players with any senior hockey experience and Frank Moores and myself felt it would take a couple of years before we would be ready to enter senior hockey," recalled George Faulkner. "But that year, we played an exhibition game in Grand Falls to open the new stadium. Because we beat the Andcos 7-3, we felt we could be competitive with most of the teams."

The imminent closure of the Bell Island iron ore mines was also a hot topic around the hockey circles in 1959 as 500 miners were laid off. Many of the island's top hockey players had to move elsewhere to find employment, thus removing Bell Island as one of Newfoundland's hockey powers.

Despite the hardship facing Bell Island off the ice, the Islanders didn't let that hamper their on ice performance in the eastern senior "B" playoffs as they defeated Conception Bay in three straight games. Bill MacDonald and Lloyd Sheppard fired two goals apiece in an opening game 8-1 victory, while Mike Fitzpatrick and Gerry Taylor each had two goals for an 8-2 win. Bill MacDonald added two more goals in the third game, won 9-3 by Bell Island, for the series sweep.

Bell Island did lose several key players when the time came to face St. John's in the eastern final. Two goals from Doug Squires enabled the Capitals to take the opening game 7-2, while three-goal performances from Doug Squires and Charlie Walsh helped win the second game 12-0. Ray Bowe and Jim Byrne each scored twice and Merv Greene stopped 27 shots for the shutout. Charlie Walsh, Joe Murphy, Bud Duffett, Ray Bowe and Doug Squires scored in a 5-2 triumph as the Caps won in three straight games.

In another off-ice development, Alex Faulkner became embroiled in a scuffle with a Carbonear player during a game in Conception Bay. Faulkner was charged and found guilty of assault and was fined $10 in court in Harbour Grace.

Gander opened the western semi-final with an 8-4 victory over defending champion Grand Falls as John Murphy netted three goals and set up two more by Cy Hoskins. The Flyers went up two games by winning teh second game 6-1 as Bill Ireland notched a pair of tallies. Grand Falls got back in the series in game three as Vic Grignon scored five goals in a 13-2 decision. Reg Ryan and Doug Budgell each added a pair. Reg Ryan netted four goals and Clobie Collins added two as Grand Falls evened the series with an 8-3 decision. The Bees completed the comeback by winning game five 6-1 with Clar Goulding firing a pair of goals.

"It took us a while to get going in that series, but we got great goaltending from Mun Pond to come back and beat Gander," stated Walt Davis. "Ray Lacroix was coaching that year and he really got us ready for the playoffs."

Hugh Wadden scored two goals in overtime to lead Buchans to a 6-4 win over Corner Brook in the opening game of their western semi-final. The big red-headed forward connected for three more goals in the second game and Roy Mullins added two as

Hugh Wadden Buchans won 7-5.

Buchans manager Gus Soper and players Hugh Wadden, Tony Head, Bob O'Toole and Norm Higdon had a near brush with death when their plane crashed in the wilderness on the return trip to Buchans. Bad weather caused their single-engine plane to ice up and crash in the woods in an attempt to land on Hind's Lake on Sunday morning. It wasn't until 4:30 Monday afternoon that their signal fire was spotted and they were rescued and taken safely to Buchans. Gus Soper received head lacerations after banging into the windshield on the crash, but the other players and pilot escaped unharmed

When the series resumed in Buchans, George Aucoin, Francis Walsh, Gerald Dwyer, Jake Critch and Joe Iannarelli scored single goals as Corner Brook stayed alive with a 5-2 win. The Royals evened the series with a 4-1 decision in the fourth game as Mickey Walsh, Dave Brake, Gerald Dwyer and Jake Critch tallied once each. The Miners rebounded in the deciding game as Jim Hornell's overtime goal earned them a 3-2 victory and a berth in the western final against Grand Falls. Frank Walker and Roy Mullins also scored for Buchans, while Dave Brake and Bob Colbourne replied for Corner Brook.

Grand Falls opened the best-of-five provincial semi-final with a 7-6 overtime win over Buchans as Heber Rideout and Clar Goulding each scored a pair of goals. Clobie Collins netted the winner in overtime and singles came off the sticks of Jim Temple and Neil Knight. Jim Hornell scored three for the Miners who got singles from Roy Mullins, Hugh Wadden and Tubby St. George. Rookie Gar Pynn scored five times as Grand Falls went two games up with a 10-5 victory. Frank Walker replied three times for Buchans.

Grand Falls seemed to have the series wrapped up as they led game three 6-1 after two periods, but Hugh Wadden had other ideas. He scored the final three goals of the third period to tie the game and connected for two more in overtime as Buchans slipped past Grand Falls 8-6. But Heber Rideout scored three times and Clobie Collins had two more as the Bees advanced to the provincial final with a 10-4 victory. Jim Hornell and Hugh Wadden each scored twice for Buchans.

Former Toronto Maple Leaf player and coach Howie Meeker was behind the bench as the Capitals opened the championship with a 7-3 win over Grand Falls with Jim Byrne scoring a pair of tallies. The Capitals went two games up the next night

as Don Yetman netted two goals in a 7-6 decision. Gar Pynn replied twice for the Bees.

Vic Grignon scored twice to lead the Bees to a 6-2 win in game three, but the Capitals regained a two-game lead with a 10-5 victory in the fourth game. Don Yetman and Jack Withers each scored three times and Stan Breen added a pair for the Capitals. Jim Temple and Reg Ryan each scored twice for the losers. Grand Falls won the fifth game 8-2 as Clobie Collins scored three goals and Clar Goulding added two. They seemed to have tied the series with a 7-1 victory in game six, but the Capitals protested the game over a penalty call. The NAHA upheld the protest and ordered the game to be replayed the next night. The second crack at game six went into overtime before Vic Grignon and Clar Goulding scored to give Grand Falls a 5-3 vistory. Jim Temple, Clobie Collins and Reg Ryan also scored for Grand Falls, while Jack Withers, Bern Goobie and Jim Byrne replied in a losing cause.

Jim Temple

"That was a great game," recalled Bob Molloy, a player with the Bees who served as general manager for the Grand Falls teams in the late 1970s and 1980s. "It wasn't decided until Clar Goulding shot the puck into an empty net from his knees inside our blueline."

The Capitals weren't very happy with the refereeing in the series or the treatment they received from the Grand Falls fans so they requested neutral referees and a neutral site for the deciding seventh game of the series. When both requests were turned down by the Newfoundland Hockey Association, the Capitals left Grand Falls and returned home, thus defaulting the series and handing the Telegram Trophy to Grand Falls.

In senior "A" action, Alex Faulkner was firing on all cylinders as the Conception Bay CeeBees played Bell Island in their first effort at the Herder Memorial Trophy. He had three goals and an assist in an opening 6-2 decision and added four goals and three assists as the CeeBees won the second game 8-4. Nev Pike backed him up with two goals, while Bill Norcott scored twice for Bell Island. Two-goal performances by Alex Faulkner, who also had three assists, George Faulkner, Kev Pike and Brian Wakelin led Conception Bay to a 9-5 victory in game three. Joe Byrne led the Islanders with three goals.

The western semi-final produced scores akin to football as the powerful Grand Falls Andcos clobbered the Corner Brook Royals by a combined score of 63-9 in the three games. Playing-coach Ray Lacroix, a native of Amos, Quebec, led the way with five goals in a 15-0 romp, while Terry Jesseau, Tom Blackmore, Alfie Hiscock and Sam Gregory each notched a pair. In the second game, Alfie Hiscock and Sam Gregory were the big shooters for Grand Falls in a 26-2 win with four goals apiece. The winners connected for 15 goals in the second period. The Andcos completed the sweep with a 22-7 verdict in the final contest. Ray Lacroix, Terry Jesseau, Alfie Hiscock, Bob Snow and Tom Blackmore each scored three times. Sam Gregory led all scorers in the series with seven goals and 13 assists for 20 points, while Ray Lacroix tallied 11 times and added seven helpers for 18 points. Alfie Hiscock and Terry Jesseau each collected 14 points.

In the opening game of the Herder final, the CeeBees got five goals and two assists from Alex Faulkner and a pair of goals from Brian Wakelin to surprise Grand Falls 9-8. Bob Snow led the losers with three goals, while Sam Gregory and Ray Lacroix each added a pair. Ray Lacroix's second goal of the game in the second overtime period earned Grand Falls a 6-5 decision in game two. Sam Gregory also scored twice, while Alex Faulkner netted three goals for the CeeBees.

Sam Gregory, Bob Snow and Tom Blackmore each scored twice as Grand Falls stopped the Conception Bay club 9-4 despite three goals from Alex Faulkner. The Andcos went up three games to one as Alfie Hiscock fired four goals and Sam Gregory had three in a 9-4 decision. Markie Andrews fired a hat-trick and Sam Gregory and Buck Hannaford had two apiece as the Grand Falls club won its fifth straight Herder with an 8-3 win. Alex Faulkner had two goals for the losers. Alex Faulkner and import Sam Gregory were the top players for their respective teams. The speedy Conception Bay forward led all scorers with 14 goals and seven assists, while Sam Gregory totalled 10 goals and six assists.

This season also marked the end of the senior "B" series with the proposal to have the senior hockey association operate a province-wide league in 1960. Grand Falls, Corner Brook,

Buchans and Gander would enter from the West, with St. John's, Bell Island and Conception Bay playing in the East. The NAHA was entering a new era that would see many ups and downs over the next 30 years as teams entered and left the senior circuit, dictated by the financial costs to ice competitive teams in Newfoundland senior hockey.

Teamwork...

is one of the most
important lessons
anyone can
learn.
That's why we
at Irving Oil
are proud to
support atheletes in
Atlantic Canada.

IRVING

**Where service
means everything.**

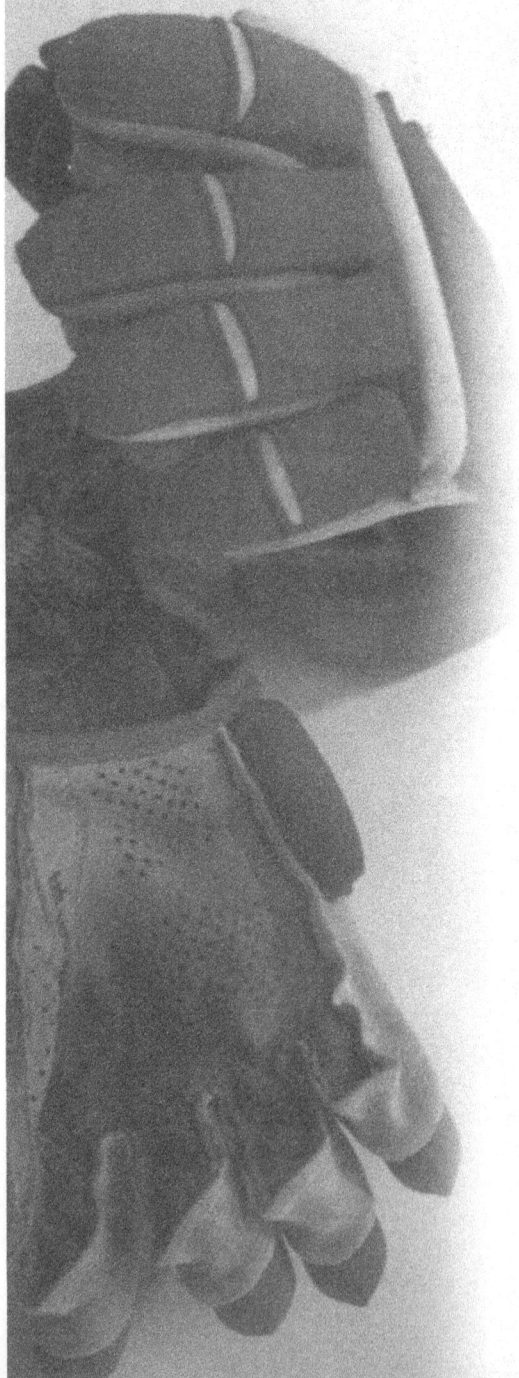

DON CHERRY'S

**THE ULTIMATE
SPORTS GRILL**

is pleased

to be a sponsor

of the first book in

OUR SPORTS HERITAGE.

290 Freshwater Rd.

(709) 596-2583

Faulkners Show the Way

The two-division format in the east and west began in 1960 as the Newfoundland senior hockey league developed into a province-wide operation. Each team played games in their respective regions before the winners advanced to the Herder Memorial Trophy playoffs. Grand Falls topped the western standings with nine wins in 12 games, while Buchans had five victories and Corner Brook and Gander garnered three apiece. Frank Finlayson of Buchans turned in the best individual effors in the division with a five-goal game against Gander and a record-setting six-goal outburst against the same team later in the season.

The eastern division was dominated by the Conception Bay CeeBees and the duo of Alex and George Faulkner. The Conception Bay squad won all eight games against Bell Island and St. John's to advance to the Herder final. Bell Island won four games, leaving the Capitals winless. Alex Faulkner tallied 25 goals and added 29 assists in eight games for an amazing total of 54 points, while brother George connected 14 times and added 21 assists for 35 points from his defence position. Included in Alex's accomplishments was a nine-point effort (four goals and five assists) against Bell Island and a record-setting seven-goal scoring spree against St. John's that broke the mark established by Frank Finlayson earlier in the season. George Faulkner also established a record for defencemen that year by scoring four goals in a 7-4 win over St. John's.

Former Grand Falls general manager Bob Molloy was often asked who was the best player he had ever seen in Newfoundland senior hockey and he simply responded by saying "Faulkner. On any given night, both George and Alex would dominate a game," he commented. "It was almost as if they would take turns controlling the game. They were the best and there's no doubt about that."

The final produced some of the best hockey ever seen in Newfoundland. Don Smith's second goal of the game in overtime gave Grand Falls the opening win as they nipped the

CeeBees 5-4. Jim Temple, Mac Davis and Clobie Collins also scored for the winners. Alex Faulkner had three and Jim Kennedy managed one for the losers. Alfie Hiscock pulled the trigger on five goals, George Faulkner netted a pair and Alex Faulkner chipped in with a goal and four assists as Conception Bay rallied for an 8-5 win in the second game. Don Smith, Mac Davis, Roger Dean, Buck Hannaford and Jean Pichette replied for the Andcos.

George Faulkner

Bill "Buck" MacDonald, added from Bell Island, scored three times, Alex Faulkner had two goals and four assists and Jim Penney, Fred Rossiter and George Faulkner had singles as the CeeBees won game three 8-6. Jean Pichette paced Grand Falls with three goals, Buck Hannaford added two and Clobie Collins sniped one. The Andcos tied the series with a 6-4 verdict in overtime on goals by Don Smith and Buck Hannaford. It was Smith's third and Hannaford's second of the game. Heber Rideout had one. Alex Faulkner had two for the losers, with single tallies coming from Alfie Hiscock and Jim Penney.

Alfie Hiscock, George Faulkner, Frank Fleming and Carl Penney scored single goals in the CeeBees' 4-3 win in the fifth game to take a 3-2 series edge. Hannaford, Jim Barker and Jean Pichette replied for the losers. An outstanding six goal and six assist effort by Alex Faulkner in the deciding game paved the way for the CeeBees to win their first Herder with a convincing 16-3 decision. Alfie Hiscock added four goals and Jack Faulkner netted three. George Faulkner had two goals and five assists and Jim Penney added a single. Jean Pichette, Neil Knight and Don Smith scored for Grand Falls, which had its five-year Herder Trophy streak come to an end.

1961

The CeeBees opened defence of their Herder Trophy championship in 1961 without their brightest star as speedy forward Alex Faulkner moved to the professional ranks. Alex Faulkner was signed to a professional contract by the Toronto Maple Leafs and began the year with the Rochester Americans of the

American Hockey League. The defending champions, with out-standing efforts from Alfie Hiscock, playing-coach George Faulkner, and former Bell Islanders Bern Fitzpatrick and Mike Kelly, continued their dominance in the eastern playoffs.

"I remember Mike Kelly and myself driving to Harbour Grace for the first time," recalled Bern Fitzpatrick. "We had to check in at the fish plant to get our money. Well, Alfie was a better player than Mike or myself and he got $70 a week. Mike was better than me and he got $65 and they paid me $60.

"That was pretty good money for playing hockey back then, but we had to earn it," said Bern Fitzpatrick. "We prac-ticed twice a day and stayed at a boarding house in Harbour Grace."

Bern Fitzpatrick began his senior hock-ey career in the late 1950s with Bell Island and played one year with Gander before signing on with the CeeBees. He was instru-mental in having Bell Island rejoin the NAHA in 1965 before moving to a professional career in the rugged East Coast Hockey League in Virginia. He also played senior hockey in Ontario before joining the St. John's Capitals. He was captain of the Capitals during their 1973 Herder champi-onship year, his final year in the senior league. He went on to coach his Bell Island club in the Conception Bay South league before evenrually retiring from the game.

Bern Fitzpatrick

The league continued its two division format and the CeeBees opened the sched-ule by taking four games from Bell Island and two from St. John's as Hiscock turned in three four-goal games. When St. John's travelled to Bell Island with only nine players and lost 5-4, they were eliminated from playoff con-tention, leaving the CeeBees to represent the east in the Herder final.

In the west, the Gander Flyers were led by playing-coach Angie Carroll and forward Fred Burke as they won their final two games of the regular schedule to tie the Corner Brook Royals for top spot with 8-4 records. Grand Falls was third at 5-7, while the Buchans Miners won only one of their 12 games. A special playoff was held between the Flyers and the Royals to determine the champion, with the Flyers edging Corner Brook 2-1 on goals by Gerry Hancock and Lester Kelly. Orin Carver replied for the Royals. The highlight of the season in the western division happened during a weekend series in Buchans when Corner Brook's import goalie John Madinsky blanked the Miners twice, stopping 69 shots in a 4-0 win Friday and making 55 saves the following night in a 1-0 victory.

Angie Caroll

The CeeBees were firing on all cylinders in the best-of-seven final and showed no mercy to the hapless Flyers. Three-goal performances by Jack Faulkner, Mike Kelly and Carl Penney lifted the CeeBees to a 13-6 decision in the opening game. Bern Fitzpatrick added two goals for the winners, with singles coming from Alfie Hiscock and Jim Penney. Fred Burke continued to lead the Flyers with five goals and Bob Dean added a single. Bern Fitzpatrick notched four goals and Jack Faulkner added three as Conception Bay hammered out a 14-4 victory in the second game. Carl Penney and Alfie Hiscock each netted a pair, while single makers came off the sticks of Mike Kelly, Jim Coady and Allan Dawe. Lester Kelly had two for Gander and Fred Burke and Bob Dean had one apiece.

Mike Kelly scored five times, while Alfie Hiscock and Jack Faulkner had two each as the CeeBees rolled to a 13-4 win in game three. Alfie Hiscock also added three assists, while Carl and Jim Penney, along with Don Pierce and George Faulkner, had single markers. Fred Burke notched a hat-trick for the Flyers and Pat Shallow scored once. The CeeBees repeated as Herder champions with a 10-4 victory in the fourth game for a sweep of the Flyers. George Faulkner led the winners with four goals, while Alfie Hiscock and Jim Coady added two apiece. Jack Faulkner and Bern Fitzpatrick chipped in with one each. Fred Burke and Angie Carroll had two each for the losers.

1962

With the taste of the Herder final so close the previous year, the Corner Brook Royals attempted to strengthen their lineup for the 1962 playoffs by adding perhaps the best mainland player to play in Newfoundland senior hockey. The arrival of Frank "Danky" Dorrington in Corner Brook propelled the Royals into a perennial contender for the Herder during his 14-year career. The new playing-coach, a native of New Glasgow, teamed with imports Doug Hillman, Orin Carver and Clobie Collins, along with goalies George John Boljkovac and Madinsky, to give the Royals potent offensive and defensive weapons as they sought their first Herder Memorial Trophy since 1935.

Before signing with the Royals, Frank Dorrington completed a two-year stint with Johnstown Jets of the Eastern Hockey League. Prior to that, he played junior hockey in New Brunswick and senior hockey in Ontario.

Despite a powerful lineup, the Royals had to defeat the Buchans Miners in the final game of the round robin schedule to claim a berth in the final. Two-goal efforts by Bob Smith and Fred Rendell lifted the Royals to a 5-3 win and a 10-2 record. The Miners fell short at 9-3, while Gander won four times and Grand Falls had one victory in 12 games. In the east, only Bell Island and Conception Bay entered the playoffs and the CeeBees swept past Bell Island in four straight games to advance to the final.

Frank Dorrington

Upon winning two games at home by 9-4 and 12-3 counts, the CeeBees got eight goals apiece from Jim Penney and George Faulkner to win two games on the island by 12-8 and 10-7 scores. Bell Island led the fourth game 7-5 with less than 10 minutes to go, but George Faulkner moved up to the forward line and pumped home five goals in less than nine minutes to seal the victory for the CeeBees.

The victory gave the CeeBees the Evening Telegram Trophy which was put up for the first time for the winner of the eastern division. Previously, it had gone to the winner of the senior "B" division. The S.E. Tuma Trophy, donated by the Corner Brook jewellery firm, was awarded to the western division champion.

The CeeBees rallied with seven goals in the third period to force overtime and won the opening game of the final 10-9 over Corner Brook on Jim Penney's goal in the second overtime period. George Faulkner paced the winners with three goals and three assists, little brother Jack tallied four times and Jim Penney's overtime goal was his third of the game. Doug Hillman, Frank Dorrington and Orin Carver each scored twice for the Royals, while Bob Smith, Clobie Collins and Fred Rendell added singles.

The Royals used a seven-goal third period to trounce the CeeBees 8-2 to even the series. Frank Dorrington and Bob Smith led the way with two goals each and singles came from Ed O'Quinn, Mike Brothers, Jim Grant and Francis Walsh. George Faulkner netted both goals for the losers. Doug Hillman scored five times and added three assists, while Frank Dorrington netted three goals and set up four more as Corner Brook took the series lead with a 15-5 decision. Clobie Collins and Mike Brothers chipped in with two goals apiece and Orin Carver, Bob Smith and Francis Walsh had singles. Jack Faulkner scored three times in a losing cause and George Faulkner and Harold Stanley had one each.

Orin Carver and Doug Hillman tallied three times each for the Royals who took an 8-6 win for their third victory of the Herder final. Ed O'Quinn and Bob Smith chipped in with single markers. George Faulkner was the bright spot for the CeeBees with two goals and two assists. Singles came from Jack Faulkner, Jim Coady and Jim and Carl Penney. During this game in Harbour Grace Pike's Hotel was burned to the ground. Having lost about $3,000 in personal belongings in the fire, the Royals were moved to accommodations in St. John's for the remainder of the series.

George Faulkner had another two-goal and two-assist night and Jim Penney scored three times as the CeeBees staved off elimination with an 8-6 victory in game five. Jim Coady, Jack Faulkner and Harold Stanley had a goal each. Doug Hillman led the Royals with two goals and singles came from Dick Power, Frank Dorrington, Ed O'Quinn and Clobie Collins.

The Royals wrapped up their second Herder Memorial Trophy the following night with a 6-1 win to take the series four games to two. With three goals, Clobie Collins was the big shooter for the Royals. Singles came off the sticks of Doug Hillman, Willis French and Fred Rendell. Jack Faulkner scored the lone goal for the losers. Doug Hillman emerged as the top scorer in the playoffs with 13 goals and six assists for 19 points, while George Faulkner fired 10 goals and set up six more. Orin Carver and Frank Dorrington had 15 points apiece.

1963

The Buchans Miners, who hadn't won a Herder Trophy in 10 years, dipped into the player marker in the off-season and came up with a formidable lineup for the 1963 playoffs. They hired playing-coach Neil Amadio from Gander and lured Mike Kelly from Conception Bay to augment their club. Neil Amadio had a very successful playing and coaching career during his stay in Newfoundland. In 1955, he captained Grand Falls to the Herder Memorial Trophy and coached Bell Island to the senior "B" title the following year. He was behind the bench for St. Pat's of the St. John's league and led them to two junior titles and two Boyle Trophy senior victories from 1959-61. He was hired by the Gander Flyers in 1962 and then moved to Buchans to lead the Miners to another Herder in 1963.

Neil Amadio

The Newfoundland senior league became a truly provincial league for the first time in 1962-63 with five teams entered, each playing 16 games. Mike Kelly became the first official scoring champion in league history when he scored 28 goals and added 12 assists for 40 points, edging Frank Dorrington of Corner Brook and Jack Faulkner of Conception Bay with 36 points apiece. Hugh Wadden of Buchans had 33 and Jim Penney of the CeeBees rounded out the top five with 31 points, including 22 goals. Bill Sullivan of the CeeBees was the top goaltender with a 4.31 average, just ahead of Terry Booth of Buchans and Mun Pond of Grand Falls, each with 4.50 averages.

Buchans, Conception Bay and Grand Falls tied for first place after the regular schedule with 20 points, while Corner Brook clinched the fourth playoff spot with 12 points. The St. John's Capitals finished last with eight points. In a special playoff to decide the top three places, Jack Faulkner had a pair of two-goal games as the CeeBees knocked off Grand Falls two games to one. A five-goal effort by Mort Verbiski helped Buchans stop

Conception Bay in two straight games to claim top spot and the Evening Telegram Trophy.

The CeeBees lost goaltender Bill Sullivan in their first semi-final game with the Corner Brook Royals when Sullivan was knocked down while chasing a loose puck and suffered a fractured skull.

His loss allowed the Royals to win the opening game 6-2 as Frank Dorrington had a goal and five assists and Doug Hillman fired three tallies. In the second game, Doug Hillman notched a pair and Frank Dorrington and Clobie Collins had one each as the Royals won 4-2. The CeeBees got a two-goal effort from Mike Fitzpatrick to take a 5-4 decision in game three and they tied the best-of-five series with another 5-4

Mike Kelly

victory in game four when Mike Fitzpatrick added two more goals to offset a hat-trick by Frank Dorrington. Doug Hillman and Bob Smith each had a pair as the Royals won the series with an 8-2 decision in game five.

The other semi-final also went the limit of the series. The Andcos opened the series with an 8-2 victory as Lindy Faulkner and Al Dwyer notched two goals apiece, but the Miners took the lead with 6-4 and 7-1 victories. Mike Kelly scored five times in game three and Frank Finlayson had five assists in game four. A four-goal outburst by Jimmy Dawe led Grand Falls to a 5-2 victory in the fourth game, setting the stage for Frank Walker's heroics in game five. Frank Walker's three goals gave the Buchans Miners a 6-2 win over Grand Falls in the fifth and deciding game.

The Royals' offence proved to be too much for Buchans as the final opened in Corner Brook. The home team took the opener 7-1 as Bob Smith scored twice. Singles came from Frank Dorrington, Francis Walsh, Doug Hillman, Mike Brothers and George Aucoin. Mike Kelly scored for Buchans. Frank Dorrington tallied twice and Bob Smith and Doug Hillman had one each as Corner Brook won the second game 4-2. Mort Verbiski and Mike Kelly scored in a losing cause.

The Miners got back in the series on home ice with a 6-2 triumph as Hugh Wadden and Frank Walker scored twice apiece and Neil Amadio and Fred Pardy had singles. Frank Dorrington and Doug Hillman replied for the losers. Frank Walker scored three times and set up two goals by Mike Kelly as Buchans tied the Herder final with a 9-2 victory. Hugh Wadden, Terry Head, Frank Finlayson and Bill Lush added singles. Bob Smith and Frank Dorrington had goals for the Royals. The Miners kept coming in game five and whipped the Royals 7-1 behind the two-goal performances of Hugh Wadden, Ed Kelly and Fred Pardy. Frank Finlayson added a single. Ed O'Quinn scored for Corner Brook. Buchans made it four straight and claimed the championship by stopping Corner Brook 6-4 in game six. Frank Finlayson scored twice for the new champions who got one apiece from Ed

Jim Dawe

Kelly, Mike Kelly, Tubby St. George and Frank Walker. Frank Dorrington scored twice for the losers, while Bob Smith and Doug Hillman added one each.

1964

The Corner Brook Royals clinched first place during the 1963-64 season with 32 points, two more than the Buchans Miners. St. John's earned its first playoff berth with 26 points and the Conception Bay CeeBees finished fourth with 15. Grand Falls was out of the playoffs with 13 points and Gander managed only two wins in 20 games. The scoring championship came down to the final weekend as Don "Ducky" Barrett of the Buchans Miners, a native of Glace Bay, Nova Scotia, tallied 10 points in his final two games to edge Frank Dorrington by a single point. Don Barrett had a league-leading 36 goals and 27 assists for 63 points, while Frank Dorrington led the league in assists with 35 and potted 27 goals for 62 points. Frank Finlayson and Mort Verbiski of Buchans finished with 55 and 50 points respectively. Corner Brook's Bert Brake walked off with the goaltending award with a 3.35 average, just ahead of Buchans' Lyle Carter at 3.45. Lyle Carter, a Nova Scotia native, later went on to the National Hockey League as a goaltender for the California Golden Seals.

The semi-final series between Corner Brook and St. John's produced one of the major controversies ever to hit the Herder playoffs. The Capitals opened the series in St. John's with a 4-2 victory on goals by Bob Badcock, Mike Donovan, Orin Carver and Doug House, while Frank Dorrington and Ed O'Quinn replied for the Royals. St. John's opened a 2-0 lead in the series by winning game two 11-2 as Orin Carver and Ian Campbell led the way with two goals apiece. The Capitals attempted to fly to Corner Brook for a Friday night game to resume the series, but poor flying conditions prevented them from reaching Deer Lake. When they were forced to stay in Gander and missed the scheduled starting time for the game, the provincial hockey association awarded the game to Corner Brook.

Bert Brake

While both hockey associations were meeting throughout the weekend to try and solve the scheduling problem, the teams took to the ice Saturday night. The Royals skated away with a 9-5 victory as Frank Dorrington scored three times and Dave Pardy added a pair. The NAHA finally turned down the St. John's request to reschedule the third game on Sunday and the Capitals were ordered to return home by the St. John's Hockey League, thus forfeiting the series to the Royals.

Frank Walker and Frank Finlayson each scored three goals and Don Barrett, Bob Smith and Hugh Wadden netted two apiece as Buchans opened the other semi-final with a 14-5 decision over Conception Bay. Al Dwyer, recruited from Grand Falls, had two goals for the losers. Jim Dawe notched four goals, Jim Penney had three and John Fitzgerald added a pair as the CeeBees evened the series with a 10-4 decision. Mort Verbiski had two for the Miners. Hugh Wadden fired a hat trick, Mort Verbiski had two goals and three assists, while Bill Malone, Frank Finlayson and Fred Pardy all chipped in with two goals as the Miners crushed the CeeBees 15-5 in game three. George Faulkner had two goals in a losing cause. Don Barrett sniped three goals and four assists, Frank Finlayson and Frank Walker fired three goals each as the Miners skated to a 16-10 win to take a commanding lead in the series. Tubby St. George and

Bob Smith added two goals each. Al Dwyer led the losers with three goals, while Jim Dawe and Jim Penney added two apiece. Don Barrett scored three more goals in the deciding game which was won 6-4 by the Miners. Fred Pardy chipped in with a pair and Frank Finlayson had the other. George Faulkner and Jim Dawe had two each for the CeeBees.

Two goals by Mickey Walsh and outstanding goaltending from Bert Brake led the Royals to a 2-1 win over Buchans in the opening game of the Herder final. Mort Verbiski had the lone goal for the Miners. Buchans came out firing in the second game and skated to an 11-5 victory as Frank Finlayson netted three goals and Frank Walker had two. Neil Amadio, Bob Smith, Tubby St. George, Hugh Wadden, Mort Verbiski and Don Barrett had one each. Mickey Walsh fired three more goals for the Royals and Jake Critch and Frank Dorrington had one each.

Frank Dorrington's three goals led Corner Brook to the series lead with a 5-2 win. Jake Critch and Francis Walsh also scored. Bob Smith had both Buchans goals. The Miners tied the series again with a 3-2 decision with goals from Don Barrett, Hugh Wadden and Bell Island native Gordie Butler. Jake Critch and Frank Dorrington replied for Corner Brook. Single goals by Ray Murphy, Harry Katrynuk, Clobie Collins and Mickey Walsh earned Corner Brook a 4-1 decision in the fifth game. Hugh Wadden scored for Buchans. The Royals claimed their first Herder Trophy at Humber Gardens with a 6-2 victory in the sixth and final game on goals by Harry Katrynuk, Frank Dorrington, Mickey Walsh, Jake Critch, Hec Caines and Dave Pardy. Frank Walker and Hugh Wadden scored in a losing cause.

Mort Verbiski

1965

The senior hockey league lost one member, regained another and welcomed home a hockey hero as the 1965 playoffs got under way. The St. John's Capitals, still at odds with the NAHA over the decision to award a playoff game to Corner Brook the year before, didn't enter competition, but Bell Island rejoined the chase for the Herder after a prolonged absence.

On the ice, the Conception Bay CeeBees welcomed home scoring star Alex Faulkner after his two productive years with the Detroit Red Wings of the National Hockey League. He was met by motorcades and dinners throughout the province, and quickly picked up where he left off in the senior league. In the 20-game schedule, Alex Faulkner tallied 22 goals and added 57 assists for 79 points to win the scoring title by two points over Frank Dorrington. The Royals' playing-coach had a league-leading 41 goals and added 36 helpers for 77 points. George Faulkner of the CeeBees had 19 goals and 44 assists for 63 points, one ahead of teammate Jim Dawe. Terry Matthews of the CeeBees was the league's top goaltender with a 3.50 average.

The CeeBees lost only two games all year and finished in first place with 35 points, two more than Corner Brook. Buchans was third with 20 points and Grand Falls clinched the final playoff spot with 16. Gander improved from the year before and won five games, while Bell Island won only twice in 20 tries.

Fan interest was at an all-time high during the decade as each club carried plenty of supporters on the train trips for weekend games. While the trips provided lots of entertainment for the fans and support for the teams, there were also some scary moments as witnessed by one incident involving a Corner Brook fan on a return trip from Grand Falls.

Dave Wheeler, a 27-year-old avid fan from Corner Brook, was late for the departure of the Royals' train from Grand Falls station to Corner Brook. As the train was pulling away, Wheeler jumped aboard, only to discover that he was on the wrong side of the car. He was trapped outside the railway car for 35 minutes before he was discovered. Wearing only one glove, he had to hang on in -17 degree temperatures and suffered severe frostbite to his ears and the fingers of one hand. He was rushed to the hospital in Grand Falls and then transferred to hospital in Corner Brook. He later had the hand removed.

Frank Dorrington, Ed O'Quinn and Clobie Collins scored the goals as the Royals opened the semi-finals with a 3-2 win over Grand Falls. Andy MacDougall and Ralph Cook scored in a losing cause. Frank Dorrington and Mickey Walsh each fired three goals and singles came from Harry Katrynuk, Ed O'Quinn and Willis French as the Royals won the second game by a 9-3 score. Jim Aylward had two for the losers and Ralph Cook added his second of the playoffs. Frank Dorrington netted two goals in the third game, a 7-2 victory. Mickey and Francis Walsh, Harry Katrynuk, Ed Lawrence and Jake Critch had one each. Al Bargery and Al Dwyer scored for Grand Falls. The Royals completed the sweep with an 11-4 decision as Mickey Walsh scored three times. The Royals got two-goal performances from Francis Walsh, Jake Critch and Ed O'Quinn and singles from Ed Lawrence and Clobie Collins. Jim Temple had two for the Andcos and Dan Malone and Andy MacDougall chipped in with singles.

Buchans got off on the right foot in the other series, surprising the CeeBees with a 7-5 victory as Hec Caines and Mort Verbiski scored two goals each. Singles came from

Mickey Walsh

Fred Pardy, Bill Malone and Jim Coady. Jack Faulkner led the CeeBees with two markers and singles came from Alex Faulkner, Jim Dawe and Harold Stanley. Jack Faulkner tallied three times, brother Alex and Gerry Lahey each netted a pair as the CeeBees stopped Buchans 8-5 in the second game. Jim Dawe had the other goal. The Buchans' markers came from Frank Walker, Hugh Wadden, Frank Finlayson, Neil Amadio and Roy Lynk. Alex Faulkner scored four times and added two assists as the CeeBees rolled to a 12-3 decision in game three. Jim Dawe chipped in with a pair.

Game four was a high-scoring affair as the Miners stopped the CeeBees 12-10. Frank Finlayson and Don Barrett each had three goals and Hugh Wadden and Hec Caines added two each. Jack Faulkner scored four times for the losers and Alex Faulkner had three more. Dawe and Alex Faulkner had two goals each in game five to give the CeeBees a 7-5 victory to take the lead in the series. Mort Verbiski replied with three goals for Buchans. Two goals by Jim Dawe led the Conception Bay club into the final with a 6-1 victory in the sixth game. Alex Faulkner led all scorers in the six-game series with 13 goals and 12 assists for 25 points, while brother Jack scored 12 times and added eight helpers. Gerry Lahey helped his club with four goals and 15 assists.

Corner Brook opened the finals with a 7-6 victory over the CeeBees as Mickey Walsh led the way with two goals. Alex Faulkner and Gerry Lahey had two goals apiece for the losers. With only 13 skaters, the CeeBees counted heavily on Alex, Jack and George Faulkner in the series. The Faulkner brothers didn't disappoint their followers.

Alex had three goals and George Faulkner, Gerry Lahey and Carl Penney had one each as Conception Bay tied the series with a 6-2 victory. Ed O'Quinn and defenceman Don Wells replied for the losers. Alex Faulkner again led the way in the third game with two goals and two assists in a 5-3 victory. George Faulkner, Jack Faulkner and Gerry Lahey added singles. Jake Critch, Clobie Collins and Harry Katrynuk scored for Corner Brook. Alex Faulkner had two goals and three assists, brother Jack fired two goals and brother George and Gerry Lahey chipped in with singles as the CeeBees took control of the Herder final with a 6-3 win. Frank Dorrington, with two, and Ed Lawrence replied for the Royals. Jack Faulkner tallied four times, George Faulkner netted two goals and added three assists and Alex Faulkner had a goal and four helpers as the CeeBees captured the Herder with a 12-5 win in the fifth game. Frank Dorrington had three and Clobie Collins netted two for the Royals. Alex Faulkner led all scorers in the final with 10 goals and 11 assists for 21 points, George Faulkner added 17, while Gerry Lahey and Jack Faulkner had 13 apiece.

1966

The 1966 Conception Bay CeeBees felt they would be hard-pressed to defend their Herder Memorial Trophy as playing-coach and team leader George Faulkner and scoring leader Alex Faulkner would be missing from the team for most of the year. George Faulkner was selected to play for Canada's national team at the World Hockey championships in Yugoslavia (where he led the team with six goals). Alex Faulkner started out with five goals and 21 points in his team's first five games, but a broken arm suffered in December put him on the shelf for the remainder of the regular season.

The rejuvenated Gander Flyers acquired the services of playing-coach Jacques Allard from Quebec, forwards Mike Kelly from Buchans, J. C. Garneau from Quebec and Doug Squires from St. John's as they became a contender for the first time. The Flyers tied for second with the Buchans Miners during the

32-game regular schedule with 34 points, 11 behind the Corner Brook Royals. The CeeBees struggled to a fourth-place finish with 28 points. The St. John's Capitals re-entered the league and finished fifth with 19 points. The change of uniform didn't affect Mike Kelly as he and Jacques Allard finished the year with 91 points apiece. Mike Kelly was awarded the scoring title on the basis of his 41 goals, one more than his teammate. Doug Squires was a distant third with 73 points, while Jim Dawe of Conception Bay had 70 and Hugh Wadden of Buchans 68. Corner Brook's Bert Brake again led all goaltenders with a 4.29 average.

Jack Faulkner potted four goals, Mac Martin added two and Alex Faulkner scored once and set up four markers as the CeeBees rolled past Gander 12-5 to open the Herder semi-finals. Ron Kelly had a pair for the Flyers. Alex Faulkner netted a pair of tallies and George Faulkner, just back from Yugoslavia, had a goal and two assists as Conception Bay won the second game 6-4. Doug Squires had two for Gander. The Flyers broke out of their scoring slump in game three as Jacques Allard had five goals

Jacques Allard

and three assists and Doug Squires netted five goals and set up two more in the Flyers' 15-7 victory. George Faulkner and Jim Penney each scored twice in a losing cause. Gerry Lahey, George and Jack Faulkner had two-goal efforts and Jim Dawe added a goal and three assists in the CeeBees' 8-2 triumph in game four. The CeeBees wrapped up the series with a 6-5 decision with George Faulkner scoring two more goals to give him seven goals and 12 assists for 19 points in the five-game series.

Buchans opened the other series with a 5-3 decision over Corner Brook as Hugh Wadden and Frank Finlayson each scored a goal and had two assists. Frank Dorrington replied twice for the Royals who evened the series with a 6-4 win in game two as Ed O'Quinn netted a hat trick and Frank Dorrington scored twice. The Royals went ahead with an 8-5 decision as Frank Dorrington, Ed O'Quinn and Jimmy Guy each had a pair of tallies. Bruce Wilson scored twice in a losing effort. Frank Dorrington and Ed O'Quinn teamed up again with two goals each to give Corner Brook a 6-3 victory in the fourth game. Buchans staved off elimination as Markie Leyte stopped 23 shots and Mort Verbiski scored three times in a 5-0 shutout for the Miners. The Royals advanced to the final with a 7-3 victory in the sixth game on the strength of two-goal performances by Mickey Walsh, Jim Guy and Ed O'Quinn.

George Faulkner tallied twice and added three assists as the Conception Bay CeeBees opened the Herder final with an 8-4 decision over the Corner Brook Royals. Mike Murphy and Jim Penney also scored twice for the winners. Bob Smith fired two goals in a losing cause. Jim Guy netted four goals and Frank Dorrington had a goal and four assists as the Royals defeated the CeeBees by the same score in game two. George Faulkner had two goals for the Conception Bay squad. Frank Dorrington scored three times and Bob Smith added a pair as the Royals forged ahead with a 9-2 victory. George and Jack Faulkner had the goals for the losers. Harry Katrynuk pulled the trigger on three markers as Corner Brook edged closer to another championship with a 7-4 decision. In the next game, Jake Critch's two goals earned the Royals the Herder as they dropped the CeeBees 7-2.

1967

The 1966-67 season marked a number of firsts for Newfoundland senior hockey. Nova Scotia native Don Johnson became the president of the Newfoundland Amateur Hockey Association and would later use this post as a stepping stone to become the first Newfoundland president of the Canadian Amateur Hockey Association. Newfoundland entered the national Allan Cup competition for the first time, while the Gander Flyers won their first Evening Telegram Trophy and Mike Kelly of Gander became the first three-time scoring champion in Newfoundland senior hockey.

The Flyers finished the season with 53 points to lead the six-team league. Conception Bay was second with 46, one more than Corner Brook. Buchans claimed the final playoff spot with 39 points, Grand Falls ended up with 33 and the St. John's Capitals were last with 24 points and only 10 victories in 40 games. Mike Kelly scored 44 goals and added 48 assists for 92 points and the scoring title. Jim Dawe of the CeeBees was second with 86 points. CeeBees' defenceman George Faulkner established a record for defencemen when he scored 35 goals and added 47 assists for 82 points to finish third. Gander's Jacques Allard had 81 points and Frank Dorrington of Corner Brook had 78. Gander goaltender Lyle Carter finished as the top goaltender with a 3.89 average.

The Flyers opened the semi-finals with a 5-4 win over the Corner Brook Royals as Pat Shallow netted two goals, including the winner in overtime. Frank Dorrington found the range twice for the losers. Jim Guy's two goals paced the Royals to a 6-4 triumph in the second game to tie the series with Jacques Allard and Cy Hoskins each scoring twice for Gander. Jacques Allard scored three times and Max Reid added two in Gander's 7-3 win in the third game. Lyle Carter kicked out 41 shots and Jacques Allard had a goal and two assists as Gander moved closer to a berth in the final with a 4-2 victory. J. C. Garneau had a two-goal night and Jacques Allard a goal and three assists to lead the Flyers to a 6-3 victory and a 4-1 series win.

Carl Penney pulled the trigger on a pair of tallies to offset two by the Miners' Don Barrett as Conception Bay opened the semi-final with a 5-4 win over Buchans, but Mort Verbiski's two-goal effort led the Miners to a 6-4 decision in the second game. Jim Penney scored twice and George Faulkner assisted three times to give the CeeBees a 4-1 victory in the third game. Jim Penney scored three goals and George Faulkner and Gerry Lahey added two each to lead the CeeBees to a 7-2 win in the next outing and they clinched a berth in the final by defeating Buchans 8-6 in the deciding contest. Bern Fitzpatrick scored four times and George Faulkner and Jim Dawe led the winners two apiece. Hugh Wadden paced the Miners with three goals and two assists.

Goals by Gerry Lahey, Bern Fitzpatrick and Carl Penney in overtime gave the CeeBees a 6-3 victory over the Flyers in the opening game of the Herder final. Gerry Lahey, George Faulkner and Peter Babb scored for the winners in regulation time, while Jacques Allard, J. C. Garneau and Ron Kelly replied for Gander. Bern Fitzpatrick and Gerry Lahey had two goals each for the CeeBees in an 8-3 win in game two. Single markers came off the sticks of George Faulkner, Jim Dawe, Carl Penney and Don Crane. Harry Katrynuk had two for Gander and Gerry Clouter added a single. George Faulkner had two goals and two assists, Jim Dawe scored twice and Bern Fitzpatrick added a goal and three helpers as the CeeBees won their third straight game with another 8-3 win. Jim Penney, Gerry Lahey and Carl Penney also scored. Mike Kelly had two and Jacques Allard one for Gander. Leo Kane fired his first two playoff goals and Jacques Allard had another as Gander stayed alive with a 3-1 win. Bern Fitzpatrick had the goal for the CeeBees who received a 51-save goaltending performance from Gary Simmons. The Alberta native would later play in the National Hockey League with the California Golden Seals. Gerry Lahey netted two goals and singles came from Bern Fitzpatrick, Jim Penney and Jim Dawe as the CeeBees won their fourth Herder of the decade with a 5-4 victory. Jacques Allard led Gander with three goals and Ron Kelly chipped in with one.

Jim Penney

The CeeBees became the first Newfoundland senior club to compete for the historic Allan Cup when they travelled to Moncton to play the Hawks in a best-of-five series. Members of the team that made that historic trip included goaltenders Gary Simmons and Doug Moores, Carl Penney, Jim Penney, Mac Martin, Bern Fitzpatrick, playing-coach George Faulkner, Nev Pike, Jim Hartling, Gerry Lahey, Don Crane, John Fitzgerald, Joe Hunt, Jimmy Dawe, Doug Sheppard and Peter Babb. The team was allowed four pickups for the series and added goalie Lyle Carter, defenceman Dick Power and forward Jacques Allard from Gander and defenceman Lloyd "Toy Toy" Gallant from Buchans.

The CeeBees started the competition on the right foot with a 6-4 overtime victory against Moncton in the first game with Jim Dawe and Bern Fitzpatrick each scoring twice. George Faulkner and Dick Power had one each. But the Hawks took over after that, winning the next three games by 6-2, 5-3 and 3-2 decisions. Jim Dawe and Jacques Allard had two goals each in the final three games, while singles came from Carl Penney, George Faulkner and Toy Toy Gallant.

1968

The arrival of playing-coach Nick Mickoski in Grand Falls had a rapid affect on the Papertowners as they climbed to a first-place finish during the 1967-68 hockey season. Grand Falls ended the season with 46 points and the Evening Telegram Trophy, one more than Buchans.

"Mickoski was probably the best import I ever played with," commented Al Dwyer. "He was a big, fast winger and he taught us a lot about the game."

Corner Brook and Conception Bay tied for third with 43 points and St. John's had 41. Gander fell to sixth spot with 22 points despite the record-setting scoring performance of playing-coach Jacques Allard who established records for goals (62), assists (69) and points (131) in the 40-game schedule. The top goaltender award went to Fred Janes of Grand Falls with a 3.90 average.

Nick Mickoski

Conception Bay got two goals from Gerry Lahey and a goal and two assists from Jim Dawe to defeat Buchans 4-1 to open the Herder semi-final playoffs. Single goals by Jim Dawe, Gary Dean, Jim Penney, Wally MacDonald and Kev Pike earned the CeeBees a 5-4 victory in the second game. Mort Verbiski had a pair for Buchans. Joey Andrea fired four goals and Mort Verbiski scored twice as the Miners started their comeback with a 7-4 victory in the third game. Jim Penney scored twice for the losers. Two-goal performances by Phil MacDonald, Joey Andrea and Mort Verbiski paved the way for Buchans to even the series with an 11-5 win. Jim Dawe had two goals for the CeeBees. Mort Verbiski and Phil MacDonald potted a brace of markers to give Buchans a 7-5 victory for the series lead despite a four-goal effort by Jim Dawe for the CeeBees. Roy Penney fired a hat trick as the Miners won four in a row by edging Conception Bay 6-5 to advance to the final. Phil MacDonald added another two goals for Buchans, while George Faulkner had three and Jim Penney two for the CeeBees.

The Corner Brook Royals received two-goal performances from Jim Guy and Jake Critch to upset Grand Falls 9-4 in the opening game of their semi-final. Tim Rothwell scored once and assisted on four more as the Royals went on to take a two-game lead with a 6-1 decision in game two. Grand Falls got back in the series by defeating the Royals 9-4 in the third game behind the two-goal efforts of Jim Temple, Alf Ellis and Ron Farnfield. The Royals, however, received shutout goaltending from Doug Grant in game four for a 3-0 victory and a three games to one lead in the best-of-seven series. Fred Janes turned the tables on the Royals with a shutout of his own and Ron Farnfield connected four times as Grand Falls stayed alive with a 10-0 win. The Cataracts sent the series to the limit in game six with a 3-2 victory on goals by Al Dwyer, Ron Farnfield and Dennis Kennedy. Grand Falls looked to have the series sewn up in the seventh and deciding game as they carried a 3-0 lead into the third period, but a six-goal explosion by the Royals carried the Corner Brook team to a 6-4 victory and a berth in the Herder finals. Ernie Hynes paced the winners with two goals.

The Royals got goals from Ed Lawrence, Jake Critch, Frank Dorrington, Ernie Hynes and Reg Asselin to nip Buchans 5-4 in the opening game of the Herder final. The Miners had two from Phil MacDonald and singles from Mort Verbiski and Leroy Clow. Phil MacDonald scored four times and goaltender George Mercer made an amazing total of 72 saves as the Miners tied the series with an 8-6 victory. Roy Penney, Mort Verbiski, Paul McWilliams and Don Lane also scored for the Miners. Ernie Hynes led the Royals with two, while singles came off the sticks of Jim Guy, Joe Lundrigan, Alex King and Reg Asselin. Jim Guy netted two goals and Reg Asselin, Foster Lamswood and Bobby Clarke had singles as the Royals took the series lead with a 5-3 verdict. Joey Andrea, Frank Finlayson and Phil MacDonald scored for Buchans. Frank Dorrington tallied twice, while Bob Clarke and Ernie Hynes chipped in with singles to lead Corner Brook to a 4-1 decision in game four. Joey Andrea had the lone Buchans goal. The Royals wrapped up their fourth Herder in seven years with a 6-4 overtime win in the fifth game with Alex King scoring twice. Singles came from Frank Dorrington, Bob Clarke, Jake Critch and Jim Guy. Phil MacDonald had two for the Miners who got one apiece from Mort Verbiski and Hugh Wadden. Frank Dorrington led all playoff scorers with nine goals and 15 assists for 24 points, while Phil MacDonald collected 15 goals and eight assists for 23 points and Mort Verbiski had 11 goals and the same number of helpers for 22 points.

With the win, the Royals advanced to the Allan Cup playoffs against the Morrisburgh Combines, the Ontario representative. The Herder champions added goaltender George Mercer from Buchans, George Faulkner from Conception Bay, along with Jacques Allard and Harry Katrynuk from Gander.

Two-goal efforts from Ernie Hynes and Reg Asselin were the only scoring the Royals could muster in a 7-4 loss to the Combines in the opening game of the series. But George Faulkner netted three goals and Ernie Hynes, Harry Katrynuk and Jake Critch added singles as the Royals tied the series with a 6-4 win in game two. Reg Asselin scored twice, while Harry Katrynuk and Jacques Allard chipped in with singles as the Royals took the lead with a 4-1 victory. The Royals became the first Newfoundland team to win an Allan Cup series when they blasted the Combines 10-0 in game four behind the 19-save goaltending effort of Doug Grant. Jacques Allard was the offensive star with three goals and five assists, while Ernie Hynes and Harry Katrynuk added two goals each. Jacques Allard led all scorers in the series with 12 points, while Harry Katrynuk had 10 and George Faulkner nine. The Royals advanced to the next series against the defending Allan Cup champions, the Victoriaville Tigers, and quickly fell behind as the Tigers posted 15-1 and 9-2 victories in the opening two games in Quebec. The Royals managed to get one win at home, 6-1 with Reg Asselin and Jacques Allard each scoring twice, but the Tigers eliminated the Royals 3-0 the following night.

1969

Gander Flyers rebounded from a last-place finish the year before to claim the Evening Telegram Trophy for the 1968-69 season with 57 points. Buchans finished second with 43, Grand Falls had 41, one more than the St. John's Capitals who knocked the defending Herder champions Corner Brook Royals out of the playoffs by two points. Conception Bay was sixth with 21 points. Jacques Allard of Gander continued his torrid scoring for the Flyers and established a new assist mark. He assisted on 76 goals, breaking his record of the previous year, and added 50 goals to finish with 126 points to claim the scoring title. Frank Dorrington of Corner Brook was second with 102 points, while J. C. Garneau of

Doug Squires

Gander was third with 80, teammate Jack Faulkner totalled 70 and Doug Squires Squires of St. John's was fifth with 65 points. Fred Janes of Grand Falls repeated as the league's top goaltender with a 3.70 mark.

The Albert "Pee Wee" Crane Memorial Trophy, named in honour of a former sportswriter at the Evening Telegram who was killed in an automobile accident in 1967, was awarded for the first time to the rookie of the year in the Newfoundland senior league. The initial winner was Grand Falls defenceman Terry French who scored four goals and collected 11 assists for 15 points in 30 games during the regular season.

St. John's opened the semi-final series with Buchans at Memorial Stadium and posted two wins over the visiting Miners. John McCallum's two goals and a single by Derm Connolly led the Capitals to a 3-2 victory in the opening game, while Phil MacDonald had both Buchans goals. Derm Connolly had two more and singles came from Doug Squires, John McCallum and Mike Fitzpatrick as the Caps won the second outing 5-2. Pierre Belanger netted both Buchans' goals. Injuries played a big part in the remainder of the series as the Caps travelled to Buchans with several regular players on the injured list. The Miners had three goals each from Frank Finlayson, Phil MacDonald and Toy Toy Gallant to take the third game 14-5. Joey Andrea and Roy Penney had two each for the winners. Paul McWilliams and Joey Andrea each scored twice as Buchans tied the series with a 5-1 decision. Pierre Belanger fired two goals in Buchans' 6-2 victory in the fifth game and the Miners wrapped up the series by stopping the Caps 7-1 in the deciding contest. Paul McWilliams scored two goals for the winners.

Playing-coach Nick Mickoski fired two goals and set up two more as Grand Falls Cataracts upset Gander 7-5 to open their semi-final. Ron Farnfield and Al Dwyer also scored twice for Grand Falls, while Jacques Allard scored twice for Gander. Brian Rafuse made 32 saves, while Jacques Allard and defenceman Stan Cook each scored twice as Gander blasted the Cataracts 10-0 in the second game. J. C. Garneau added a goal and three helpers for the Flyers. Jacques Allard and J. C. Garneau each contributed three goals to lead Gander to a 9-4 verdict to take the series lead with Gary Dean netting two for Grand Falls. The Flyers received goals from Jacques Allard, Stan Cook, Jack Faulkner and Leo Kane to edge Grand Falls 4-3 in game four. Jim Temple had two and Roger Martin one for Grand Falls, who stayed alive in the series with a 4-2 victory in the fifth contest as Al Dwyer scored twice and Ron Farnfield and Roger Martin connected. Jacques Allard and J. C. Garneau replied for Gander. The Flyers got a goal and three assists from Mike Kelly on their way to a 6-1 win over Grand Falls and a berth in the finals in the sixth game. Other goal scorers for the winners included Ed Philpott, J. C. Garneau, Jack Faulkner, Leo Kane and Jacques Allard. Ralph Cook scored the lone Grand Falls goal.

J. C. Garneau and Pat Shallow each scored twice as Gander won the opening game of the finals with a 7-3 victory over Buchans. Harry Katrynuk, Leo Kane and Ed Philpott also tallied for the winners, while Frank Finlayson, Mort Verbiski and Joey Andrea replied for Buchans. Jacques Allard had three markers and singles came off the sticks of Leo Kane, Pat Shallow, Bill Lastic and Mike Anderson as Gander took the second game 7-1. Joey Andrea had his team's only goal. The Flyers doubled Buchans 10-5 for a 3-0 lead in the series as Leo Kane netted three markers and Jack Faulkner added two. Singles came from J. C. Garneau, Ed Philpott, Jacques Allard, Mike Anderson and Bill Lastic. Frank Finlayson had two for the Miners who had singles from Pierre Belanger, Roy Penney and Joey Andrea. Brian Rafuse stopped 37 shots and the Flyers received goals from Jack Faulkner, Mike Kelly, Pat Shallow, J. C. Garneau and Leo Kane to wrap up their first Herder Memorial Trophy with a 5-0 shutout. Jack Faulkner was the top scorer in the playoffs with seven goals and 18 assists for 25 points, while Jacques Allard had 14 goals and 23 points. He was followed by J. C. Garneau with 20, Mike Kelly with 19 and Leo Kane with 15.

The Flyers added goaltender Doug Grant from Corner Brook, Leo Murphy and Al Dwyer from Grand Falls and George Faulkner from Corner Brook for their Allan Cup series with the Galt Hornets. (George Faulkner had been hired to manage Humber Gardens and play for the Royals.) The

Jack Faulkner

Hornets won the best-of-seven series in five games, although the Flyers were close in all but one outing. Leo Kane had two goals in an opening 4-3 loss, while Mike Anderson and Mike

Kelly each had two as Gander dropped the second game 7-4. J. C. Garneau netted two goals in Gander's lone win, a 5-4 decision, while Bill Lastic had two goals in a 6-4 setback. Galt won the other game 9-1.

The decade also brought about an end to the participation of the Conception Bay CeeBees in the provincial league. Faced with increasing costs for players, the CeeBees called it quits after 11 years, winning four Herder Memorial Trophies during that span. The CeeBees, stocked with players from all over the province, were one of the top drawing cards in the senior league and provided plenty of thrills and first-class entertainment for hockey fans throughout the province.

Congratulations

from

Bidgood's SUPERMARKET

*A Modern day supermarket
full of delightful memories*

ain Highway

oulds

ewfoundland

709) 368-3125

**Proud supporters of hockey
in the Goulds and on the
Southern Shore for many years.**

PLAY IT AGAIN SPORTS

516 Topsail Road
(709) 745-7529 • 1-800-830-7529

Proud Sponsor

of

OUR SPORTS HERITAGE

We Buy, Sell, Trade and Rent

Used and **New**

Sporting Goods.

Sports Equipment That's Used,
But Not Used Up

St. John's Teams Dominate

The St. John's Capitals took their level of play to new heights as the Herder Memorial Trophy playoffs entered the 1970s. The Capitals captured their first Evening Telegram Trophy as first-place finishers during the regular schedule. This triumph was an omen of things to come during the decade, as teams from St. John's went on to capture seven of ten Newfoundland senior hockey championships. In fact, the Capitals, under coach Bob Badcock, became so powerful that the senior league was having trouble attracting teams to enter the circuit. In an effort to save senior hockey in the province, the St. John's Capitals were divided into two teams in 1977. The St. John's Blue Caps and the St. John's Mike's Shamrocks became household names in senior hockey circles.

Bob Badcock

1970

The Capitals finished with 49 points during the season, six more than Gander, while Corner Brook was third with 41. Grand Falls claimed fourth place with 39 points and Buchans was in the cellar with 28. Frank "Danky" Dorrington of Corner Brook claimed his first scoring championship with 118 points on 43 goals and 75 assists, just three ahead of Gander's Jacques Allard who had 40 goals and 75 helpers for 115 points. Gander's Leo Kane was a distant third with 83 points, including a league-leading 44 goals. Jimmy Guy of Corner Brook had 80 points and Ed Philpott of Gander finished with 70. Eg Billard, the diminutive St. John's goaltender, was the top netminder in the senior circuit with a goals against average of 3.80. St. John's defenceman Bruce Butler and Buchans goaltender Cliff Piercey were named co-winners of the rookie of the year award and the Albert "Pee Wee" Crane Memorial Trophy.

The semi-final series between St. John's and Corner Brook was a real homer clash, as neither team was able to win in the other team's rink. Goals by Bruce Butler, Phil MacDonald and Roy Penney led the Caps to a 3-1 win in the series opener. Gerry Lahey, in his second season with the Royals since moving from Conception Bay, replied for the losers. Overtime goals by Mike Donovan and Jim Penney led the Caps to a 6-4 decision in the second game. Ford Metcalfe, John McCallum, Doug Squires and Bruce Butler had the other goals. George Faulkner led the Royals with a goal and three assists, while Alex Blanchard netted a pair and Jim Guy had the other. Two-goal performances by Ed O'Quinn, Bobby Clarke, Jim Guy and Frank Dorrington led Corner Brook to a 12-2 decision when the series resumed at Humber Gardens. Two goals by Frank Dorrington and one by Jim Guy, all in the third period, had the Royals even the series with a 3-1 victory. Bern Fitzpatrick had the lone St. John's goal. Frank Dorrington netted three goals and set up one by Ernie Hynes as Corner Brook took the series lead with a 4-2 decision. Bern Fitzpatrick and Phil MacDonald replied in a losing cause. The Caps got back on track as game six was played at Memorial Stadium with a 5-2 victory. George Spracklin had two goals, while singles came from Phil MacDonald, Roy Penney and John McCallum. Jim Guy and Bob Clarke had the Royals' tallies. Two-goal performances by George Spracklin and Jim Penney earned St. John's a 7-0 shutout in the seventh and deciding contest. Eg Billard stopped 25 shots for the shutout and single goals came from John McCallum, Bern Fitzpatrick and Phil MacDonald.

George Spracklin

Referee Ron Healey of Bishop's Falls, one of the more colourful characters connected with the senior league, was on the receiving end of a practical joke by Corner Brook defenceman Doug Sheppard during the series. Sheppard toiled as a barber in Corner Brook and Healey went in to get a haircut prior to the game that night. Healey was the proud owner of two very long sideburns and Sheppard shaved one off while Healey was in the chair. Healey didn't notice it until he was in the referee's room just prior to game time and was hopping mad as he chased Sheppard all over the ice during the pre-game warmup.

Harry Katrynuk scored one goal and assisted on three more as Gander opened defence of the Herder with a 7-1 victory over Grand Falls in the other semi-final series. However, playing-coach Jim Beckman had a goal and two helpers in the second game as Grand Falls edged the Flyers 5-3. Three goals by Ed Philpott and singles by Bill Lastic, Leo Kane and Jacques Allard led the Flyers to a 6-3 triumph in the third contest. Jim Temple netted two and Roger Martin had a single for the Cataracts. Gander moved to within one game of a berth in the final with a 4-2 victory in the fourth game. Goaltender Brian Rafuse made 50 saves for the Flyers who had goals from Mike Anderson, Leo Kane, Ed Philpott and Jacques Allard. Jimmy Dawe had both Grand Falls markers. Alf Ellis notched a pair of markers and Temple, Martin and Dawe added singles as the Cataracts stayed alive in the series with a 5-2 win in game five. Leo Kane scored both Gander goals. Fred Janes made 22 saves and Jim Beckman and Jim Temple each potted a pair of goals as Grand Falls evened the semi-final at three games apiece with an 8-0 decision. Al Dwyer, Jim Dawe, Roger Martin and Toy Toy Gallant also scored. The seventh game was an epic struggle that went into the second overtime period before Flyers' defenceman Bill Lastic sent the Gander crowd into a frenzy with the winning goal. The Flyers advanced to the final with a 7-6 decision. Dennis Mullins had two goals for Gander, while Leo Kane, Ed Philpott, Mike Kelly and Jacques Allard had one each. Jim Beckman and Al Dwyer each had two goals and three assists for Grand Falls who got their other goals from Jim Dawe and Alf Ellis.

Leo Kane fired three goals and assisted on Mike Kelly's marker as Gander opened the best-of-seven final with a 4-3 victory over the Capitals. Jim Penney scored twice, while Stan Cook scored a single for the Capitals. However, two-goal performances by Doug Squires and Mike Donovan propelled the Capitals to a 7-1 victory in the second game. Bill Malone, Jim Penney and Bern Fitzpatrick also scored. Jim Mullett replied for Gander. Mike Donovan had two goals and two assists and George Spracklin chipped in with a pair as the Capitals trounced the Flyers 12-2 in game three to take the lead in the series. A six-goal outburst in the third period broke a tie and

Gander tripped the Caps 9-3 to even the series at two games apiece. Leo Kane had two goals and six assists to lead the winners, while Mike Anderson and Jacques Allard had three goals and three assists apiece. Ron Kelly added the other goal. Bill Malone, Bob Badcock and Stan Cook scored for the Caps. Mike Anderson scored twice, while singles coming from Jacques Allard, Ed Philpott and Dennis Mullins as the Flyers forged into the lead with a 5-3 decision in game five. Bob Badcock, Doug Squires and Bruce Butler had the goals for the St. John's crew. Eg Billard was flawless between the pipes, kicking out 26 shots as the Capitals posted a 4-0 shutout win to tie the series at three games each. Mike Fitzpatrick, George Spracklin, playing-coach Les Calder and Bob Badcock scored the goals. Rugged winger Ford Metcalfe pulled the trigger on three goals and Doug Squires added a pair as St. John's clinched the Herder with a 7-3 win in the final contest. It was the first Herder win for St. John's since St. Bon's claimed the award in 1949. George Spracklin and Jim Penney, who was celebrating his fifth Herder Trophy, also scored goals, while Pat Penney had two for Gander and Mike Anderson had one.

The Capitals advanced to the eastern Allan Cup series against Quebec's powerful Victoriaville Tigers. The Capitals added Bill Lastic, Leo Kane and Jim Beckman to bolster their lineup for the series at Memorial Stadium in St. John's. Jean Guy Morrissette, who would later star in the Newfoundland senior league, made 37 saves as the visiting Tigers edged the Capitals 6-5 in overtime to open the best-of-five series. Jim Beckman, Ford Metcalfe, Bern Fitzpatrick, John McCallum and Les Calder scored for the Caps. Jean Guy Morrissette came back in the second game with a 34-save performance as his mates doubled St. John's 4-2. Les Calder and Jim Beckman were the St. John's marksmen. Goals by George Spracklin, Jim Penney and Leo Kane led the Capitals to their only victory in the series, a 3-1 decision. The Tigers wrapped up the affair with a 7-3 victory in the fourth game as the losers got goals from George Spracklin, Jim Penney and Jim Beckman.

1971

The 1970-71 senior hockey season will best be remembered for three things: Claude Anstey assumed the presidency of the NAHA when Don Johnson moved up to the ranks of the Canadian Amateur Hockey Association; St. John's, Corner

Brook, Grand Falls and Gander played a meaningless 36-game regular schedule; and, perhaps most memorable of all, the St. John's Capitals collapsed in the final against the Grand Falls Cataracts.

St. John's repeated as winners of the Evening Telegram Trophy with 42 points, while Corner Brook was second with 39, Grand Falls had 33 and Gander finished fourth with 30. Instead of playing regular semi-finals, the league decided to put all four teams into a home-and-home round robin semi-final. From this series, Grand Falls emerged in the lead with a 9-3 record, while Gander and St. John's both finished at 6-6. The Caps got second place by virtue of defeating the Flyers three out of four times in the semi-final. The Flyers had a chance to finish second with a win over Corner Brook in their final game, but Royals' goaltender Doug Grant blocked 59 shots and the Flyers lost 5-3. The Royals finished fourth with only three victories in 12 outings. Jack Faulkner of Gander captured the scoring title with 74 points, one more than brother Alex who toiled with the Capitals. Corner Brook's Ernie Hynes was third with 71 points, while defenceman Hubert Hutton of St. John's followed with 69 points, including a league-leading 49 assists. Capitals' Eg Billard repeated as the top goalie with a 3.94 average, while Corner Brook forward Bram Pike received the most votes as the rookie of the year. Jack Faulkner and teammate Ed Philpott were the top point-getters in the semi-final series with 27 apiece, while Alex Faulkner was next with 25.

Hubert Hutton collected a goal and three assists and Derm Connolly chipped in with a pair of goals as the Capitals opened the final with a 5-2 victory over Grand Falls. Doug Squires and Bern Fitzpatrick also scored. Jim Temple and Al Dwyer scored for Grand Falls. Hubert Hutton fired two goals, while singles came from Doug Squires and Alex Faulkner to lead St. John's to a 4-0 win in the second game. Eg Billard stopped 19 shots to post the shutout. The Capitals took a stranglehold on the best-of-seven series with a 4-2 victory in the third contest as George Spracklin had a pair of goals and Derm Connolly and Bern Fitzpatrick chipped

Hubert Hutton

81

in with one apiece. Jim Beckman and Jimmy Dawe replied for the Cataracts. The monumental comeback for Grand Falls started in game four as they defeated the Capitals 5-2 behind the two-goal performance of Al Bargery. Al Dwyer, Frank Finlayson and Jim Temple scored singles. Derm Connolly and Alex Faulkner answered for the Capitals. Goaltender Jean Guy Morrissette, signed by Grand Falls from Victoriaville, had to make only 15 saves as Grand Falls won their second game 8-0. Jim Dawe had two goals and two assists, while Al Bargery scored once and set up three more. Roger Dwyer, Frank Finlayson, Al Dwyer, Jim Beckman and Alf Ellis added singles. Two goals from Roger Bowers led Grand Falls to a 7-1 victory to tie the series at three games apiece. Jim Dawe, Frank Finlayson, Al Dwyer, Jim Temple and Alf Ellis added singles. Jack Hill replied for the Capitals. With Jean Guy Morrissette making 29 saves for his second shutout of the series, the Cataracts completed the comeback with a 3-0 decision in the seventh game on goals by Frank Finlayson, Jim Dawe and Roger Bowers.

Jack and Alex Faulkner and Bern Fitzpatrick were added to the Grand Falls roster as they took on the Galt Hornets of the Ontario Hockey League in the eastern Allan Cup series. Galt opened the series with a 4-2 win as Jim Beckman and Alf Ellis scored in a losing cause. Alex Faulkner netted two goals and assisted on two by Jim Beckman as the Cataracts evened the series with a 6-3 decision. Jim Dawe and Jack Faulkner also scored. Jack Faulkner, Jim Dawe and Bern Fitzpatrick scored in the third game, but it wasn't enough as Grand Falls fell 5-3 to Galt. However, Jean Guy Morrissette stopped 43 shots, including a penalty shot, to lead Grand Falls to a 3-1 victory in game four as Al Dwyer, Alex Faulkner and Jim Dawe netted the goals. Jean Guy Morrissette, the series MVP, was outstanding in the final game as well, but his mates fell 6-3 to a more experienced Galt team. Jack Faulkner had two goals and Jim Dawe one for Grand Falls.

1972

As good as Jean Guy Morrissette was in his initial year with the Cataracts, he was even better in 1971-72. During the regular season, the former professional goaltender with the Montreal Canadiens set a record for goaltenders with a 2.33 goals against average from 77 goals against in 33 games. In the three-team round robin playoffs, he lowered that to 2.25, giving up 18 goals in eight games. And his performance in the final against St. John's was even more remarkable as he gave up only six goals in four games for a 1.50 mark with one shutout.

"Morrissette was in a class all by himself when it came to goaltending," recalled Bob Molloy. "He made saves that other goaltenders would find impossible. It seemed he got better as the games became more important. In that series against St. John's when we came back with four straight wins, he was absolutely remarkable."

Al Dwyer also felt that there were many great goaltenders in the senior league, "Gary Simmons was great with the CeeBees and Gander had Lyle Carter," said Dwyer. "Doug Grant of Corner Brook was the best local goaltender and Tols Chapman played well for St. John's, but Morrissette was the best goaltender that ever came into the province. "

Jean Guy Morrissette led Grand Falls to first place and the Evening Telegram Trophy during the season, while St. John's was second and Gander third. Corner Brook finished out of the playoffs. The Cataracts swept through the semi-final with eight straight victories, while the Capitals clinched second with a 3-5 mark and Gander had only one win. Gander playing-coach Wayne Maxner led all scorers with 52 goals and 59 assists for 111 points, well ahead of teammate Jack Faulkner who totalled 68. Bobby Clarke of Corner Brook was third with 62 points, two better than Alex Faulkner of St. John's with 60. Don Howse of Grand Falls was voted rookie of the year as he scored 23 goals and added 18 assists for 41 points. He also had an eight-point game on four goals and four assists in a semi-final game against Gander.

Grand Falls opened the final against St. John's with a 7-1 victory with Jim Beckman and Jim Munch each scoring two goals. Don Howse, Leo Murphy and Al Dwyer had one each. George Faulkner scored for the Capitals. Al Dwyer registered a hat-trick, while Jim Beckman, Tony Grimes and Jim Dawe chipped in with singles to lead Grand Falls to a 6-0 victory in the second game. Jean Guy Morrissette was forced to make

Leo Murphy

83

only 12 saves to record the shutout. Jim Temple netted a pair of markers and singles came off the sticks of Al Bargery, Jim Munch and Al Dwyer as the Cataracts won the third game 5-3. Jack Hill, George Spracklin and Hubert Hutton were the St. John's marksmen. The Cataracts swept to the Herder with a 5-2 triumph in the fourth game as Frank Finlayson scored twice and singles came from Terry French, Jim Temple and Jim Munch. George Spracklin and Derm Connolly replied for the Capitals.

The Cataracts earned the right to meet the Barrie Flyers of Ontario in the eastern Allan Cup competition and added Alex Faulkner, Jack Faulkner, Les Calder and goaltender Doug Grant to their lineup. But the Grand Falls club was no match for the Barrie Flyers who swept the best-of-seven series in four straight games. Jim Dawe potted two goals in an opening-game 3-2 loss and Jack Faulkner and Jim Munch replied as the Cataracts lost 8-2 in the second game. Les Calder notched the lone goal in game three, a 4-1 loss that saw Jean Guy Morrissette injured. Al Bargery and Al Dwyer had the goals for Grand Falls in a 6-2 setback in the final contest.

Doug Grant left the provincial senior ranks following this season and joined Memorial University where he backstopped

the Beothucks to their first-ever playoff spot. From his play at the Atlantic college championships in Halifax, he was scouted by the Detroit Red Wings and signed a professional contract with the club. Grant was an all-star with Virginia Red Wings in the American Hockey League before graduating to the National Hockey League with the Detroit Red Wings and later with the St. Louis Blues.

Jean Guy Morrissette retired after his stint in Newfoundland, but he never forgot his time in Grand Falls. "The people of Grand Falls were just great and the Newfoundland senior hockey league had some of the best amateur players in Canada," he said. "I really enjoyed my time there."

Doug Grant

1973

After losing eight consecutive playoff games to Grand Falls, the St. John's Capitals cleaned house and brought in plenty of new faces for the 1973 Herder playoffs. Under the guidance of rookie coach Bob Badcock, the young team nicknamed the "Kiddie Korps", weren't expected to fare well against the more experienced teams in the senior loop. The Capitals hovered around the .500 mark during the regular season and won five straight games in the round robin semi-final to clinch a berth in the final. The Capitals really caught fire in the final and swept past Grand Falls in four straight games to clinch the Herder Memorial Trophy. Corner Brook rebounded from a last-place finish the year before to clinch the Telegram Trophy with 37 points, 10 more than the Capitals. Grand Falls had 35 and Gander was eliminated with 25. Frank Dorrington of Corner Brook claimed his second league scoring crown with 67 points, two more than Al Dwyer of Grand Falls. Linemates Jim Guy and Ernie Hynes of the Royals followed with 63 and 61 points respectively. Jack Faulkner of Gander was next with 56. Rocky Martin of Grand Falls claimed the goaltending honours with a 4.14 mark and the top rookie was Gary Connolly of the Capitals who established a new mark with 31 goals and 50 points.

The round robin semi-final was a thrilling race to the finish. After six games, all three teams were tied at 2-2 before the Capitals took two games from Grand Falls and one from Corner Brook to gain a berth in the final. An overtime goal by Frank Finlayson earned the Cataracts a 5-4 win over Corner Brook for the second berth in the final. Derek Hancock led the Capitals with three goals and Charlie Greene added a pair in an opening-game 8-2 victory over Grand Falls. Nigel Facey, Ford Metcalfe and Bob Hutton also scored for the winners. Tony Walsh and Alf Ellis had the Grand Falls goals. Jerry Power, Hubert Hutton, Derm Connolly and Randy Pearcey scored for the Capitals in a 4-2 decision in the second game. Frank Finlayson and Al Bargery scored for Grand Falls. Randy Pearcey, Derek Hancock, Sandy Gibbons and Bern Fitzpatrick had a goal each as St. John's nipped Grand Falls 4-3. Harry Katrynuk had two goals and Al Bargery scored one for the Cataracts. Ford Metcalfe, Derek Hancock and Randy Pearcey scored in the final game as the Capitals swept to the Herder with a 3-1 victory. Harry Katrynuk had the Grand Falls goal. Frank Dorrington was the top overall scorer in the playoffs with 19 points, while

Randy Pearcey totalled 15 and Frank Finlayson had 14. Capitals' goaltender Doug Atkinson led all performers with a 3.36 average.

Randy Pearcey joined the Capitals for their playoff drive after completing an outstanding career with the Memorial University Beothucks in Atlantic intercollegiate hockey. He became the sparkplug and team leader for the Capitals during the decade where he became the team's top scorer. The feisty centreman used his great skating ability and hockey sense to overcome his lack of size and became the first native-born player to score 50 goals in a single season in the senior league.

Harry Katynuk

"Getting a chance to play for the Capitals has to rate as my greatest thrill in hockey," he said. "Growing up in the rink, I watched the Caps get beaten a lot of times. It was a great accomplishment to be part of a Herder championship team." Before he retired in 1985, Pearcey collected five Herder titles with the Capitals and also performed with the Gander Flyers and the Stephenville Jets.

The Capitals ran into a powerful Thunder Bay Twins team in Allan Cup play. After splitting the first two games, the Twins turned on their offence in the next two games to take the series three games to one. Derm Connolly, Nigel Facey, Randy Pearcey and Hubert Hutton each scored in a 6-4 loss, while Sandy Gibbons accounted for two goals and Nigel Facey, Rick Babstock, Randy Pearcey and Bern Fitzpatrick one each in the Caps 6-3 victory. Bern Fitzpatrick and Sandy Gibbons scored in a 6-2 setback and the Caps were blanked 9-0 in the fourth game.

1974

The Capitals continued to dominate the regular season and 1974 Herder playoffs. They lost only four games in the 32-game regular season to finish with 55 points, well ahead of Grand Falls who had 38. Corner Brook followed with 30, while Gander was fourth with 20 and the first-year Clarenville Caribous managed 17 points. Little Dave Oxford of Corner Brook established a record for first-year players when he scored six goals and had four assists in one game against Gander. He finished the year with 24 goals and 44 assists for 68 points to win the Albert "Pee Wee" Crane Memorial Trophy. The Royals' Frank Dorrington repeated as the scoring champion with 33 goals and 68 assists for 101 points, while Al Dwyer of Grand Falls was a distant second with 69, one more than Dave Oxford. Charlie Greene of Grand Falls had 56 points and Ernie Hynes of the Royals was fifth with 54. Tols Chapman of the Capitals was the league's top netminder with a 3.53 average and two shutouts

Two-goal performances by Charlie Babstock and Hubert Hutton led St. John's to a 7-1 win over Corner Brook to open semi-final play. Tols Chapman made 20 saves in the second game as the Capitals blanked the Royals 3-0. Sandy Gibbons contributed three goals and Brian Brocklehurst added a pair as St. John's raced to a 3-0 series lead with an 8-3 victory. Frank Dorrington had two goals for the losers. Rookie Bill Perry notched four goals and Paul Althouse had two as Corner Brook posted a 9-1 win in the fourth game, but two goals by Derek Hancock, including the winner in overtime, gave the Capitals the series with a 5-4 victory.

Al Dwyer was named the first winner of the Howie Clouter Memorial Trophy, awarded to the most gentlemanly and effective player in the league. It was donated by the Clouter family in memory of their son Howie, a former player with the Gander Flyers, who was killed accidentally. Al Dwyer had an outstanding series in the semi-final with the Gander Flyers. The veteran centreman had his best-ever offensive output in the five-game series with ten goals and 11 assists to pace the Cataracts.

"I was just in the right place at the right time and I had lots of help", the quiet Al Dwyer stated.

He connected for four goals and four assists to lead Grand Falls to a 14-1 win over Gander in the opening game. Jim

Al Dwyer

Munch chipped with three goals, while John MacSween and Charlie Greene added two apiece. Al Dwyer had three more goals in the second game as the Cataracts slipped past the

Flyers 7-4. Fern Garneau and Don Harvey had two each for Gander. Charlie Greene, Al Dwyer and Ross Flood had two goals apiece and Harold Stanley had a goal and five assists as Grand Falls won the third game 8-7. Jack Faulkner scored twice for Gander. Jack Faulkner and Gary Mitchell had two goals apiece as Gander staved off elimination with a 7-4 victory in game four. Charlie Greene scored twice in a losing cause. The Cataracts advanced to the final by trouncing the Flyers 15-4 in the fifth game on the strength of three-goal efforts by John MacSween, Roger Martin and Harry Nichols. Ross Flood added a pair and Al Dwyer had a goal and four helpers.

Charlie Babstock pulled the trigger on four goals as the Capitals opened the best-of-seven Herder final with a 7-6 win over Grand Falls. Charlie Greene was tops for the losers with two goals and two assists. Charlie Babstock, Max Hayes and Sandy Gibbons each had two goals and Sandy Gibbons added four assists as the Capitals crushed the Cataracts 10-2 in the second game. But two goals and two assists from Jim Munch enabled Grand Falls to stop the Capitals 5-2 in game three. Brian Brocklehurst was the triggerman on two goals as St. John's edged closer to the Herder with a 6-2 victory. The Capitals wrapped up the championship with a 6-1 verdict in the fifth game as Bob Hutton and Randy Pearcey each had a goal and two assists. Al Dwyer was the top scorer in the playoffs with 11 goals and 14 assists for 25 points, Jim Munch had 19, Charlie Greene and Sandy Gibbons had 17 apiece and Leo Murphy of Grand Falls had 16. Tols Chapman led all goaltenders with a 3.30 average and one shutout.

The Capitals advanced to the Allan Cup series against Thunder Bay, but lost three straight games. Tols Chapman made 40 saves in the opener as the Caps lost 4-3 with goals coming from Nigel Facey, John McCallum and Derek Hancock. Sandy Gibbons and Max Hayes had goals in the final two games, both 9-1 losses to the powerful Twins.

1975

The Newfoundland Senior Hockey league saw the lowest number of teams to ever compete for the Herder Trophy in 1975 with only three communities entering play. The St. John's Capitals finished first with 26 points, the Grand Falls Cataracts had 18 points and the Corner Brook Royals managed one victory and two ties in 16 games. In an effort to generate more money, and confident that they would win the series, Grand Falls offered to play Corner Brook in a best-of-three semi-final, with the winner advancing to meet the Capitals in the Herder final. But the Royals stunned the Cataracts in two straight games and won 6-5 and 7-6 in overtime. Frank Dorrington led the Royals in the opening game with two goals, while John MacSween and Al Dwyer had two apiece for the Cataracts. Alex Blanchard and Bill Crocker fired two goals each for the Royals in the second game and Terry Gillam netted the overtime winner.

The Capitals received goals from Randy Pearcey, Brian Mulcahy, George Faulkner and John McCallum to open the final with a 4-3 victory. Al Matthews, Terry Gillam and Alex King replied for the Royals. Goals by Randy Pearcey, Sandy Gibbons, Ed James, Nigel Facey and John McCallum provided St. John's with a 5-1 margin of victory in the second game. Denis Woolfrey had the lone Corner Brook goal. Bob Faulkner, George's son, and Erik Seaward led the Capitals to a 10-4 decision in game three with two goals each. Singles came from Sandy Gibbons, John McCallum, Greg Pearcey, Randy Pearcey, Max Hayes and Jim Heale. Ralph Dunne, Terry Gillam, Frank Dorrington and Alex Blanchard had the goals for the Royals. The Capitals swept to the Herder with a 6-2 victory in the fourth game as Ed James scored three times and singles came from Dan Noftall, John McCallum and Randy Pearcey. Denis Woolfrey and Jim Roche scored for Corner Brook.

Charlie Greene of Grand Falls was the league-scoring champion with 46 points on 10 goals and 36 assists, while Glen Critch of St. John's, the rookie of the year winner, was next with 37 points. Al Dwyer of Grand Falls finished third with 34 points and was the Howie Clouter award winner for the second consecutive season. Tols Chapman of St. John's repeated as the league's top goaltender with a 2.63 average.

Frank Dorrington, who had planned to retire a year earlier, was coaxed out of retirement to play in the series for the Royals. He officially announced his retirement after the Royals were defeated and left as the all-time top scorer in Newfoundland senior hockey. During his 14-year career, the veteran centreman scored 360 goals and added 551 assists for 911 points during regular season play, capturing three scoring championships and four Herder Memorial Trophies along the way.

The Capitals advanced to Allan Cup competition against Dalhousie Tigers of New Brunswick and opened the best-of-five series with a 14-4 victory. Glen Critch paced the win with three goals and Randy Pearcey had two goals and three assists. Rick Babstock netted a pair of tallies. Randy Pearcey was back in the second game with two goals and two assists as the Capitals took a 9-1 victory. They swept the series with a 12-3 win as Charlie Babstock scored three times and Glen Critch added two.

The next series against Ontario's Barrie Flyers displayed some of the dirtiest and roughest hockey ever played at Memorial Stadium in St. John's. The Flyers won the opening game 8-4 as Glen Critch, George Faulkner, Charlie Babstock and Randy Pearcey scored the goals. But a vicious crosscheck to the back of the head of Capitals' defenceman Bob Lambert precipitated a bench-clearing brawl. The second game, won 6-5 in overtime by Barrie, wasn't as rough, but provided plenty of heavy hits and was an indication of what was to break out in the third game. Ed James had two goals and two assists, while Glen Critch, Nigel Facey and Charlie Babstock scored in a losing cause for the Capitals.

A series of fights broke out late in the first period of the third game played on a quiet Sunday afternoon. Every player on the ice was fighting and, when the dust had settled and the Capitals had won just about every battle going (to the delight of the 4,100 howling fans at the stadium), the Flyers limped off the ice and refused to return. The game was awarded to St. John's. But the Flyers regrouped for the next game and won 4-3 with John McCallum scoring two goals and Charlie Babstock adding one for the Capitals.

1976

The senior league played an unbalanced schedule for the 1976 Herder Trophy as only four teams entered competition. Grand Falls, Corner Brook and Stephenville competed in the west and played 20 games, while the St. John's Capitals were the only eastern entry and played 12 times. The standings were computed on a percentage basis and the Capitals claimed the Evening Telegram Trophy with 18 of 24 possible points for .667. Grand Falls finished second at .650, Corner Brook was third with .550 and Stephenville was fourth at .200 after winning only eight of 40 possible points. Gene Faulkner of Grand Falls became the first rookie in NAHA history to win the scoring title as he had 17 goals and 22 assists for 39 points. But he didn't win the rookie of the year award. That went to Stephenville's Cal Dunville who was third in scoring with 31 points. Jim Guy of Corner Brook was second with 38 points, while Brian Jesso of Stephenville and Alex Blanchard of the Royals also had 31 points apiece. The top goaltender was Pat Dempsey of St. John's with a 3.83 average and teammate Hubert Hutton was named winner of the Howie Clouter award as the most gentlemanly and effective player.

Corner Brook and Stephenville opened the playoffs with a best-of-five quarter-final series. Gary Peddle netted two goals and Jim Guy had a goal and three assists as the Royals won the opening contest 7-3, but the Monarchs rebounded with a 7-4 victory to tie the series with Cal Dunville netting three goals and two assists and Nish Dobbin sniping a pair. Cal Dunville had a goal and four helpers and Nish Dobbin chipped in with two more goals as Stephenville nipped the Royals 6-5 in overtime to take the lead in the series. Terry Gillam had two goals for the losers. Cal Dunville scored three times and assisted on four markers as Stephenville eliminated Corner Brook with a 10-5 decision. Gerry Stride had four goals for the winners, while Jim Guy had two in a losing effort.

Grand Falls got two-goal performances from Alex Faulkner and Roger Grimes to defeat Stephenville 11-2 to open the semi-finals. Three goals by Alex Faulkner and two each from Gene Faulkner and Leo Murphy enabled the Cataracts to win the second game 8-6 despite a three-goal and three-assist performance from Cal Dunville. Roger Martin was the big sniper in game three as he fired three goals and assisted twice for Grand Falls and the Cataracts swept to the final against the Capitals with a 7-1 triumph in the fourth contest. Cal Dunville had quite a playoff run as the speedy centre scored 14 times and collected 16 assists in eight playoff contests.

Tony Grimes scored two goals and assisted on three more and defenceman Leo Murphy added a goal and three helpers as the Cataracts stopped St. John's 8-3 in the opening game of the finals. Alex Faulkner and Gene Faulkner, Denis Goulding and Harry Nichols also scored for the winners, while Max Hayes, Charlie Babstock and Jim Wilcox had the Capitals' goals. A four-goal performance by Glen Critch and two from Charlie Babstock pulled the Capitals even with a 9-4 victory. Nigel Facey, Randy Pearcey and Ed James also scored for St. John's as

Grand Falls received goals from Al Dwyer, Denis Goulding, Leo Murphy and Ross Flood. Randy Pearcey scored twice and the Capitals had singles from Charlie and Rick Babstock, Ed James and Jim Heale to stop Grand Falls 6-1. Al Dwyer replied for the losers. Randy Pearcey assisted on three goals, while Glen Critch, Brian Gibbons, Charlie Babstock and Ed James had the goals as St. John's doubled the Cataracts 4-2 in the fourth game. Denis Goulding and Ross Flood scored for the losers. The Capitals claimed another Herder Trophy with a 6-2 victory in game five as Charlie Babstock, Nigel Facey, Charlie Greene, Ed James, Jim Heale and Brian Gibbons, who performed with Springfield in the AHL and the Toronto Toros of the WHA, scored the goals. Ross Flood and Denis Goulding were the Grand Falls marksmen. The Capitals advanced to the Allan Cup playoffs against Gatineau, Quebec, and lost three games by scores of 5-2, 11-4 and 6-4. Nigel Facey, Glen Critch, Ed James and Randy Pearcey had two goals each for St. John's and Jack Gibson had the other against the Quebec champions.

1977

The senior league expanded to eight teams as the battle for the 1977 Herder began. Corner Brook topped the western division with 50 points and claimed the Evening Telegram Trophy, while Gander had 43, Grand Falls 24 and Stephenville 21. The St.

Erik Seaward

John's Capitals split their powerful team into two entries, with the Blue Caps finishing first in the eastern standings with 34 points, while Mike's Shamrocks followed with 32. Clarenville was next with 21 and Memorial University, who dropped out of Atlantic college competition to enter the senior league, had 14. Memorial's Erik Seaward was named rookie of the year as he tallied 15 goals and 21 assists for 36 points. Denis Goulding of Gander led the scoring parade with 91 points from 43 goals and 48 assists, followed by Ernie Hynes of Corner Brook with 77, Alex Blanchard of the Royals with 74, teammate Terry Gillam had 72 and Randy Pearcey of the Blue Caps with 65 points. Corner Brook's Ted McComb was the top goaltender with a 3.76 average. Gander forward Tom Rafuse was named the winner of the Howie Clouter award for sportsmanship and ability.

Kirk Johnson netted four goals, while Ed Philpott and Keith Elliott added two apiece as Gander opened the western quarter-final with a 13-3 win over Grand Falls. John MacSween scored three times and Gary Feener and Gene Faulkner had two each for the Cataracts to even the series with a 10-7 victory. Ed Philpott and Kirk Johnson had two each for Gander. The Flyers won the series with an 8-1 victory in the deciding game with Gary King and Andy Gover connecting for two goals each. In the east, John Hearn and Gary Connolly netted two goals apiece as the Shamrocks got past Clarenville 9-2. Two-goal performances by Dave Ivany and Jim Tilley, however, enabled the Caribous to tie the series with an 8-1 score. The Shamrocks advanced with a 9-5 decision as Derm Connolly scored a pair of goals. Calvin Wells had two in a losing cause.

Alex Blanchard fired two goals and added three assists and Terry Gillam chipped in with a pair of tallies as Corner Brook won the opening game of the semi-final with an 8-2 victory over Gander. Alex Blanchard added a goal and two assists in the second game as the Royals won 4-2. They wrapped up the series with a 6-3 victory as Terry Gillam notched a hat trick. Kirk Johnson had two goals in a losing effort. Charlie Babstock scored three times and Jim Mullett and Ken Cashin each had a pair as the Blue Caps tripped the Shamrocks 9-2 in the eastern series. But the Shamrocks knotted the series with a 7-4 win as Nigel Facey had two goals and Glen Critch added a goal and four assists. Two goals from Brian Mulcahy and a 27-save shutout effort from Barry Frost gave the Blue Caps a 2-0 win in game three. They clinched a berth in the final by edging the Shamrocks 3-2 thanks to Randy Pearcey's overtime goal. Tony Pearcey and Rick Babstock also scored for the winners, while Gary Noftle accounted for both Shamrocks' goals.

Corner Brook got goals from Alex Blanchard, Rick Boone, Terry Gillam, Joe Lundrigan, Jim Guy and Ernie Hynes to stop the Blue Caps 6-3 in the opening game of the final. Jim Heale, Randy Pearcey and Charlie Babstock replied for the losers. Rick Boone, Terry Gillam and Alex Blanchard each scored twice and Bill Perry had one as Corner Brook won the second game 7-4. Randy Pearcey, Charlie Babstock, Brian Mulcahy and Sandy Gibbons scored for the Blue Caps. Charlie Babstock netted three goals, Randy Pearcey had two goals and two assists and Jim Heale added a goal and three assists as the Blue Caps got back in the series with a 7-2 decision. Brian Mulcahy added the other goal. Alex Blanchard and Terry Gillam answered for the Royals. Alex Blanchard had two goals and an assist and Terry Gillam a goal and two helpers to lead the Royals to a 6-1 decision in the fourth game. Jim Guy, Bill Perry and Joe Lundrigan chipped in with one each as Charlie Babstock replied for the losers. The Blue Caps stayed alive with a 5-2 victory in game six on goals by Randy Pearcey, Sandy Gibbons, Jim Heale, Charlie Babstock and Gary Sullivan. The Royals had goals from Alex Blanchard and Paul Althouse. Corner Brook went on to claim the Herder with a 7-1 victory at Humber Gardens. Bill Perry led the way with three goals and two helpers, while Paul Althouse, Jim Roche, Terry Gillam and Alex Blanched added one apiece. Gary Sullivan had the lone goal for the Blue Caps. Terry Gillam and Randy Pearcey led all playoff scorers with 19 points apiece and Ted McComb continued his fine play between the pipes, leading all goaltenders with his 3.11 average.

Because the Capitals had split their team in an effort to maintain competition within the senior league, they were afforded the opportunity to challenge the Royals for the right to advance to Allan Cup play. In the best-of-three series at Corner Brook, Randy Pearcey and Glen Critch had two goals each and Jim Heale scored in overtime as the Capitals edged the Royals 8-7 despite a three-goal game from Terry Gillam. Defenceman Bob O'Neill netted two goals as the Capitals took the second game 5-4.

The Capitals opened the Allan Cup competition against Shediac, New Brunswick, and won the first game 7-4. Randy Pearcey and Charlie Babstock each had a goal and two assists. Randy Pearcey collected a goal and four helpers, while Jim Heale and Don Quinn each had two goals as the Capitals trounced Shediac 11-4 in the second game. But the visitors stayed alive with a 6-5 decision in the third contest. The fourth game came to an early finish. With the Capitals leading 2-0 after the first period, problems with the ice-making machine left the ice in less than perfect condition. The Shediac team refused to finish the game. Consequently, the Capitals were awarded the series.

The eastern final against the Brantford Alexanders from Ontario provided some very entertaining hockey at Memorial

Stadium. The Ontario champions easily won the first two games with scores of 9-1 and 7-4. The Capitals, however, rebounded in game three with a 9-3 victory with Terry Ryan making three goals and two assists and Jack Gibson netted two goals and helped on three more. Linemate Paul Newman also assisted on five goals. Terry Ryan and Jack Gibson scored in game four as St. John's nipped the Alexanders 2-1. However, a pair of third-period goals gave Brantford a 5-3 decision in the final game and a berth in the Allan Cup final.

1978

A record 11 teams entered competition for the Herder Memorial Trophy in 1978. The Blue Caps led the eastern division with 51 points and captured the Evening Telegram Trophy. The Clarenville Caribous and the Shamrocks tied for second with 26 points, while the Memorial Beothucks had 19 and the Bonavista Cabots managed a single point. The Gander Flyers led the western entries with 47 points, one more than the Corner Brook Royals. The Grand Falls Cataracts were third with 39 points and the Labrador City Carol Lakers claimed the fourth playoff spot with 30 points. The Stephenville Jets had 23 and the Buchans Miners managed eight points. Randy Pearcey of St. John's became the first Newfoundland-born player to score 50 goals in a single season and the first St. John's Capital to win the scoring title as he netted 51 markers and added 55 assists for 106 points to edge Kirk Johnson of Gander who had 102. Gander's Zane Forbes had 84 points, Jim Heale of the Blue Caps 64 and Terry Gillam of the Royals had 63. Pat Dempsey of the Blue Caps captured his second top goaltending award with a 3.71 average. Zane Forbes was the top rookie for the season and teammate Ted Mercer was named the Howie Clouter award winner.

"That was my biggest individual thrill, getting 50 goals," commented Randy Pearcey. "It had never been done by a local player before and it's something that always stands out in my mind." The speedy centreman "regrets" not pursuing hockey as an occupation, although he was

Randy Pearcey

approached by scouts from the St. Louis Blues and the Buffalo Sabres. "There was nobody to go with, so I never took them up on their offers," he added.

Kirk Johnson's three goals enabled Gander to open the western quarter-final with a 7-2 win over Grand Falls and he was back in game two with two goals and two assists in Gander's 11-3 romp. The Buchans native netted two goals in game three as Gander eliminated the Cataracts by a 7-3 count.

Veteran Jimmy Dawe fired four goals and added an assist as Labrador City surprised Corner Brook 9-3 in their first game. The Carol Lakers went two games up with a 10-6 decision as Jim Dawe, Adrian Sullivan and Bill Lake had two goals. Playing-coach Joe Lundrigan fired a goal and four assists. (Joe Lundrigan, a native of Corner Brook, also performed in the professional ranks with Rochester of the AHL and had a short stint with the Toronto Maple Leafs.) Bill Perry tallied four times for the Royals. Alex Blanchard had two goals as the Royals won the third game 4-2, but Jim Dawe scored three times, leading the Carol Lakers to a 7-3 victory in the fourth game to eliminate the Royals.

In semi-final action, Kirk Johnson and Jim Mercer each had two goals, with Zane Forbes collecting a goal and three assists, as Gander won the opening game 10-1 over the Carol Lakers. Zane Forbes had two goals in an 8-2 victory in game two and both he and Kirk Johnson notched a goal and two assists as Gander won the series with a 5-2 decision.

Jim Tilley's two goals earned Clarenville a 7-3 win over Memorial University in the eastern playoffs. Dave Ivany had a goal and three assists as the Caribous won the second outing 3-1. Calvin Wells fired two goals as Clarenville eliminated the Beothucks with a 7-1 decision.

Bob O'Neill had two goals and an assist in the Shamrocks' 4-3 win over the Blue Caps in their series, but Charlie Babstock scored three goals as the Blue Caps tied the series with a 6-2 triumph. Charlie Babstock had two goals, including the winner in the third overtime period, as the Blue Caps nipped the Shamrocks 3-2. Bob O'Neill notched both goals for the losers, who evened the series in game four with a 4-1 victory. Two goals by Derek Hancock paved the way for the Blue Caps to win the series with a 5-1 victory.

The Blue Caps had a rather easy time in the next series with Clarenville. Jim Heale notched two goals in an opening 5-2 win and Mike O'Handley scored two goals as the Blue Caps took the second game 8-1. Randy Pearcey netted four goals and Sandy Gibbons, Jim Mullett and Charlie Greene had three goals each as the city team clobbered the Caribous 15-0. Pat Dempsey made 21 saves for the shutout.

The best-of-seven final between the Gander Flyers and the Blue Caps proved to be one of the most entertaining in the history of the senior championships. The Flyers came to Memorial Stadium and got three goals from Tom Rafuse to upset the home team 9-6. Kirk Johnson and Zane Forbes each added a pair of markers and Reg and Doug Batson chipped in with singles. Rick Babstock fired a pair for the losers who got singles from Randy and Tony Pearcey, Jim Mullett and Don Quinn. Charlie Greene fired three goals, Gander native Ed Philpott had two and singles came from Charlie Babstock, Jim Heale, Tom Kinsella and Don Quinn as the Blue Caps tripped Gander 9-2 in the second game. Doug Batson and Dennis Laing had the goals for Gander. The games turned into high-scoring affairs when the series resumed at tiny Gander Gardens. Gary King scored three times and singles came from Keith Elliott, Gerry McCarron, Kirk Johnson and Jim Mercer with Gander taking a 7-1 win. Tony Pearcey scored in a losing cause.

Gander looked to take a commanding lead in the fourth game when the Flyers built up a 5-0 lead after one period and led 7-2 heading into the third frame. But a spirited comeback by the Blue Caps saw them rally to tie the game at 7-7 after regulation time and pull out a 10-9 decision in overtime. Ed Philpott and Jim Heale led the comeback victory with three goals and two assists each, while Randy Pearcey had two goals and singles came off the sticks of Sandy Gibbons and Charlie Greene. Gary King and Zane Forbes had three goals and three assists each for the Flyers who also received a goal and five assists from Kirk Johnson. Keith Elliott and Jim Mercer also scored. The Flyers had two-goal efforts from Gary King and Tom Rafuse, a goal and five assists from Zane Forbes and a goal and three assists from Kirk Johnson to trounce the Blue Caps 12-3 for the lead in the series. Jim Wooder, Reg and Doug Batson, Don Harvey and Paul Sweeney also scored for Gander. Derek Hancock, Ed Philpott and Sandy Gibbons were the goalscorers for the losers.

Two-goal performances by Derek Hancock, Sandy Gibbons and Jim Heale gave the Blue Caps an 8-6 overtime victory in game six. Erik Seaward and Jim Mullett also scored. Bruce Sparkes, Doug King, Don Harvey, Jim Mercer, Keith Elliott and Doug Batson had the Gander goals. Charlie Babstock's goal late in the third period proved to be the winner as the Blue Caps nipped the Flyers 4-3 to capture the Herder Memorial Trophy. Jim Heale, Charlie Greene and Jim Mullett had the other goals, while Gerry McCarron, Zane Forbes and Doug Batson replied for the Flyers. Kirk Johnson led the playoff scorers with 36 points, including 15 goals, while Zane Forbes followed with 35 and Randy Pearcey had 30. Pat Dempsey led all playoff goalies with a 3.48 goals against average. The Blue Caps advanced to the Allan Cup playoffs in Brantford, Ontario, but managed only one win with Ed Philpott scoring three times in an 8-5 victory. The Newfoundland club lost 11-3, 10-4 and 8-1 in the other games.

1979

The 1978-79 hockey season began like any other for Mike's Shamrocks. But before it was over, players and supporters of the green and gold club would experience a season they would never forget. The Gander Flyers and the Blue Caps were given the edge to meet again in the final as both teams finished the season with 43 points. Gander won the Evening Telegram Trophy on the basis of a better record. The Shamrocks were next with 32 points, Corner Brook had 28 for fourth place, Grand Falls was fifth with 23, while Stephenville managed 11 points. Ed Philpott returned to Gander and established a new assist record with 79 to go with his 47 goals for a total of 126 points and the scoring title. He also picked up the Howie Clouter award as the most gentlemanly and effective player. Teammate Jim Mullett was a distant second with 81, Randy Pearcey of the Blue Caps had 72, Dave Ivany of Gander 67 and Jim Heale of the Blue Caps 58. Pat Dempsey of the Blue Caps was the league's top netminder for the second straight season with a 4.02 average. Mike's Shamrocks' defenceman John Breen was named rookie of the year and winner of the Albert "Pee Wee" Crane Memorial Trophy.

The Shamrocks and the Blue Caps would meet for the third season in a row in the playoffs, with the Blue Caps winning both previous series. This time, the Shamrocks were looking for revenge. With the strains of Sister Sledge's "We Are Family" motivating the rag-tag hockey club, the Shamrocks opened the semi-final with a 3-1 victory over the Blue Caps as Bill Perry, John Hearn and Jerry Power scored the goals. Glen Critch replied for the losers. Randy Pearcey had four goals and four assists, Charlie Babstock and Jim Heale added two goals and three assists each as the Blue Caps humbled the Shamrocks 12-2 in the second game. Glen Critch also had two for the winners and John Hearn had both Shamrocks' markers. A hard-fought 3-2 victory in game three turned the season around for the Shamrocks who received goals from Bob Faulkner, Gary Connolly and Hubert Hutton. Randy Pearcey and Charlie Babstock scored for the Blue Caps. The Shamrocks defeated their city rivals 5-2 in the fourth game to advance to the final for the first time. John Hearn led the way with two goals and an assist as the other goals came from Gary Noftle, Ron Cadigan and Gary Connolly.

Action in the other semi-final saw Zane Forbes and Ed Philpott each score twice as Gander stopped Corner Brook 6-4. Alvin Park netted two goals for the Royals. Ed Philpott, Zane Forbes and Keith Elliott had two goals each as Gander won the second game 9-2 and Jim Mullett's pair of markers enabled the Flyers to advance to the final with a 7-3 verdict in the final contest.

Keith Elliott's goal in the third overtime period lifted Gander to a 3-2 victory as the Herder final opened in Gander. Ed Philpott and Zane Forbes also scored for the winners, while Bill Perry and Ron Cadigan answered for the Shamrocks. Mark Idler's goal, with less than two minutes to play, earned the Shamrocks their first win, 4-3, in the second contest. Bob O'Neill, Bob Faulkner and Gary Connolly also had goals. Keith Elliott netted a pair for Gander and Ted Mercer chipped in with the other. The Shamrocks moved into the lead when the series resumed in St. John's with a 5-3 decision. Nigel Facey had two goals and John Hearn had a goal and two helpers. Jerry Power and John Breen had one each. Johnson, Elliott and Forbes had the Gander markers. The Flyers evened the series with a 5-3 win with Zane Forbes scoring twice. Kirk Johnson, Dave Ivany and Rick Doyle had one each. John Hearn led the Shamrocks with two and Bob O'Neill netted one. The Flyers moved ahead with a 7-5 victory in overtime in game five. Dave Ivany and Kirk Johnson led the attack with two goals and Terry Ryan, Zane Forbes and Rick Doyle added one each. John Hearn, Gary Noftle, Mark Idler, Bob Faulkner and Hubert Hutton scored for the Shamrocks. The green and gold Shamrocks kept their Herder hopes alive in the sixth game and pulled out a 4-3 victory on goals by Bill Perry, Gary Noftle, Bob O'Neill and Hubert Hutton. Ed Philpott, Keith Elliott and Zane Forbes took care of the Gander scoring.

The seventh and deciding game went into the second overtime period before Ron Cadigan's shorthanded goal, his second of the game, delighted the Shamrocks' supporters with a 6-5 victory that stunned a capacity partisan crowd at Gander Gardens. John Hearn, Gary Noftle, Paul Norman and Bob O'Neill scored for the Shamrocks, while Ed Philpott led Gander with two goals. Single markers came from Zane Forbes, Dave Ivany and Kirk Johnson. John Hearn led all playoff scorers with 10 goals and 11 assists for 21 points, three more than Ed Philpott. Rick Doyle followed with 16 points and Zane Forbes had 15. Gander goalie Terry John led all netminders with a 3.38 mark.

John Hearn

The Shamrocks advanced to the Allan Cup series and hosted Petrolia, Ontario, but managed only one victory against three defeats. Bob O'Neill's two markers gave the Shamrocks a 6-4 victory in game two, but they came out on the short end of the 5-3, 10-4 and 3-1 scores in the other games.

The dominance of the St. John's teams was evident during the decade, but the influx of top-quality imports in Grand Falls, Stephenville and Corner Brook raised the level of hockey in other centres. The St. John's Capitals would not win again until they dipped into the player market themselves eight years later.

100

The

St. John's
Junior Hockey League

and its members

St. John's Capitals
Bell Island
Celtics
Trinity-Placentia
Avalon
Southern Shore
Mount Pearl
Northeast
Conception Bay South
Conception Bay North

are proud to be sponsors

of

OUR SPORTS HERITAGE

––––––––––––––––

Congratulations

on the publication of

Herder Memorial TROPHY

the first book in

OUR SPORTS HERITAGE

from

LeGrow's Travel
We Know Travel Best.

A member of the Maritime Marlin
and Thomas Cook Group

BEST
MANAGED
PRIVATE
COMPANIES

**20 Locations in Newfoundland & Labrador
Telephone: toll free – 1 800 663 6300
Visit our web site : www.legrowstravel.nf.ca**

The Quest for the Allan Cup

While Newfoundland had been represented in Allan Cup competition since 1967, the provincial representatives hadn't fared too well. With only three series wins against Atlantic Provinces competition and one against the Ontario senior "B" representatives since that time, Newfoundland teams began to set their sights on the Allan Cup in the 1980s. While the Newfoundland senior clubs became stronger with the influx of paid players from the mainland, this great cost also initiated the demise of the Newfoundland senior hockey league. The heavy financial burden forced many teams to withdraw from the league.

1980

Gander finished first during the 1979-80 season with 52 points and maintained their hold on the Evening Telegram Trophy. The Blue Caps followed with 41 points and Grand Falls had 36. The Shamrocks claimed the fourth spot with 34 points, two ahead of Corner Brook. Stephenville was next with 17 points and Labrador City was last with 16. Zane Forbes of Gander captured the scoring title with 47 goals and 47 assists for 94 points, 10 more than teammate Dave Ivany. Randy Pearcey of the Blue Caps had 76, Kirk Johnson of Gander was fourth with 75 and Glen Critch of the Blue Caps had 70. Gander's Kevin Kelly led all goaltenders with a 3.55 mark. The top rookie was Mac Tucker of the Blue Caps with 27 goals and 34 assists for 61 points in his first season. Gander's Tom Rafuse won his second Howie Clouter award.

Zane Forbes netted three goals to lead Gander to a 6-5 overtime victory against the

Zane Forbes

Shamrocks in a rematch of the previous year's Herder final. Three-goal efforts by Zane Forbes and Keith Elliott and two each by Dave Ivany and Tom Rafuse paced Gander to an 11-3 triumph in the second game. Gander closed out the series and advanced to the final by sweeping the Shamrocks 5-3 behind the two-goal performance of Kirk Johnson.

Charlie Babstock scored two goals for the Blue Caps for a 6-5 win in game one, while two-goal efforts from Randy Pearcey and Glen Critch helped win game two 7-4 over Grand Falls in the other semi-final. Tony Walsh scored three times for the Cataracts in the second game. Two goals by Wayne Faulkner lifted Grand Falls to a 4-3 victory to stay alive in the series, but Charlie Babstock netted two goals in a 3-2 Blue Caps victory in game four to send them to the final against Gander.

Gander opened the best-of-seven final with a 6-4 victory as Zane Forbes and Ed Philpott each connected for a pair of tallies. Keith Elliott and Doug Batson chipped in with singles. Jim Heale had two for the Blue Caps who also had single markers from Glen Critch and Mac Tucker. Goals by Kirk Johnson, Tom Rafuse, Doug Batson, Keith Elliott, Dave Ivany and Ted Mercer helped Gander stop the Blue Caps 6-1 in the second game. Bob Jackman had the lone goal for the losers. Glen Critch connected twice and the Blue Caps got goals from Paul Newman, Charlie Babstock, Jim Heale and Randy Pearcey to up end Gander 6-5 in game three. Tom Rafuse, Ed Philpott, Dennis Laing, Zane Forbes and Keith Elliott (on a penalty shot) scored for Gander. Mac Tucker netted three goals, while Bob Jackman, Randy Pearcey and Charlie Babstock chipped in with singles to lead the Blue Caps to a 6-1 win in tying the series at two games apiece. Keith Elliott connected again for Gander.

Ted Mercer had two goals for Gander in a 7-2 victory in game five to retake the series lead. Singles came from Kirk Johnson, Jim Mullett, Tom Rafuse, Ed Philpott and Dave Mercer. Randy Pearcey and Rick Babstock scored the Blue Caps' goals. The Flyers clinched the Herder with a 5-1 win in the sixth game. Kirk Johnson led the winners with three goals and an assist and Zane Forbes chipped in with a goal and two helpers. Dave Ivany had the other goal. Charlie Babstock was the only Blue Caps' shooter to beat Flyer goaltender Kevin Kelly. The red-headed cagecop finished the playoffs with a 3.31 average.

Zane Forbes topped all playoff scorers with 21 points, including 12 goals. Kirk Johnson followed with 19, Randy

Pearcey had 18, Ed Philpott 15 and Glen Critch 14. Gander did-n't fare any better than previous teams in Allan Cup play as they were trounced in three straight games by the Thunder Bay Twins. The Flyers lost by scores of 9-1, 10-2 and 10-4.

1981

Import Bruce Campbell, a native of Nova Scotia who was a dominant scorer during his days in Newfoundland senior hock-ey, was named the initial winner of the T. A. "Gus" Soper award as the most valuable player in the league for the 1980-81 season. The award was presented in memory of Soper, a driving force behind the Buchans Miners during their early days and their chase for the Herder Memorial Trophy. Campbell, who played with the Corner Brook Royals, finished third in the league scoring with 42 goals and 79 points. Randy Pearcey of the Blue Caps finished first with 86 points, including 59 assists, for his sec-ond scoring title, while Zane Forbes (now with the Blue Caps) was runner-up with 83 points. Danny Flynn of Grand Falls, who won the Howie Clouter award as the most gentlemanly and effective player, was fourth with 60 points and teammate Steve

Bruce Campbell

Croucher had 47 points. The Blue Caps' goaltender Roger Kennedy won two awards. In addition to being the top goal-tender with a 4.36 average, he won 13 of his 23 starts and was named rookie of the year. Grand Falls took three of four games from the Blue Caps in the final week of the schedule to win the Evening Telegram Trophy with 43 points, followed by the Blue Caps with 41. Corner Brook finished third with 33 points, five more than the Shamrocks. Labrador City failed to make the playoffs with only nine points in 24 games.

Glen Critch scored three goals and added an assist as the Blue Caps opened their best-of-seven semi-final with a 6-2 deci-sion over Corner Brook. But the Royals got a two-goal perfor-mance from Cal Dunville to stop the Blue Caps 8-2 and even the series. Two-goal efforts by Bruce Campbell, Byron Rideout and Darren McWhirter paced the Royals to a 9-7 victory in game three as Mac Tucker and Mike Mealey each counted twice for

the losers. Byron Rideout and Bruce Campbell had three points apiece in the Royals' 7-3 win during the fourth game and Bruce Campbell was back in game five with three more goals advancing the Royals to the final with a 9-4 decision.

Gene Faulkner fired two goals and import goaltender Mark Locken stopped 29 shots as Grand Falls blanked the Shamrocks 8-0 in the opening game of their series. Gary King's overtime goal earned the Shamrocks a 3-2 victory in game two. Dan Flynn paced Grand Falls to a 5-3 win with two markers in game three, while Wayne Faulkner collected three goals and two assists leading Grand Falls to 5-1 and 4-1 victories that won the series in five games.

The Royals opened the final with a 4-3 victory on goals by Bill Perry, Terry Gillam, Darren McWhirter and Craig Kennedy. Grand Falls had goals from Tony Walsh, Gene Faulkner and Dan Flynn. Tony Kennedy, Gene Faulkner and Larry O'Donnell scored the goals as the Cataracts evened the series with a 3-1 win. Craig Kennedy had the lone goal for the Royals. Alex King and Bill Perry pulled the trigger on two goals each as Corner Brook won the third game 8-3. Steve Gallant, Cal Dunville, Terry Gillam and Bruce Campbell also scored. Dan Flynn managed with two, and Ron Sweeney scored once for the losers. Wayne Faulkner had a pair of tallies in Grand Falls' 6-2 triumph in the fourth game. Sean Jewer, Terry Head, Tom Coolen and Laurie Cuvalier had singles. Alex King netted both Royals' markers. Ron Sweeney fired two goals and singles came off the sticks of Dan Flynn, Terry Head and Roger Elliott as the Cataracts took the lead in the series with a 5-2 victory. Bill Perry and Byron Rideout scored in a losing cause. Tom Coolen netted three goals and Ron Sweeney added a pair as Grand Falls routed Corner Brook 11-0 in the final game with Mark Locken stopping 21 shots for the shutout. The highlight of the final game was a second-period heavyweight battle between Corner Brook's Steve Gallant and Grand Falls' enforcer Gordie Gallant. Both players battled on the ice for more than 10 minutes, much to the delight of the 3,000 fans at the Grand Falls Stadium.

For the first time, the Allan Cup playdowns involved a four-team round robin tournament in Thunder Bay. Grand Falls opened the event with a 3-2 win over St. Boniface, Manitoba. Larry O'Donnell, Wayne Faulkner and Terry Ryan scored the goals. The Cataracts didn't fare too well in the next two games as they were dumped 9-4 by Thunder Bay and 10-2 by Petrolia,

Ontario. The Cataracts were defeated by Petrolia, the eventual champions, 6-3 in the semi-final game as Dan Flynn, Terry Ryan and Laurie Cuvalier scored the goals.

Grand Falls native Terry Ryan had an outstanding junior career with the Hamilton Red Wings of the Ontario Hockey League before turning professional. His best years were spent with Minnesota Fighting Saints in the WHA and Minnesota North Stars of the NHL.

1982

The Gander Flyers loaded up on talent and returned to the senior league in the chase for the Herder Memorial Trophy in 1982. The Flyers won the Telegram Trophy with 43 points, two more than Grand Falls. Stephenville was third with 34, the Shamrocks had 29, while the Blue Caps collected only 16 points and failed to make the playoffs for the first time. Zane Forbes had moved from St. John's back to Gander and was named the league's most valuable player after finishing second in the scoring race with 71 points. Bruce Campbell, now with Grand Falls, won the title with 75 points and also picked up the Howie Clouter award. Steve Croucher of Grand Falls was third with 69, followed by Rick McCallum of Gander with 65 and Terry Ryan of Stephenville with 59. Jim Mercer of Gander was the league's top rookie, scoring 32 goals and adding 25 assists for 57 points, while the goaltending award went to Ed Davis of Grand Falls with a 4.02 average.

Don Howse

Darren Pickrem scored three goals, while Zane Forbes and Tom Rafuse each had two goals and two assists as Gander stopped the Shamrocks 11-4 to open semi-final action. Jeff Andrews pulled the trigger on a pair of goals with Gander winning the second game 6-1. Former Blue Cap Randy Pearcey scored in overtime and John Phillips added a pair of goals as Gander eliminated the Shamrocks with a 7-6 decision. John Hearn and Jim Heale each scored twice in a losing cause.

Bruce Campbell had two goals as Grand Falls opened their semi-final with a 4-2 win over Stephenville. Ron Sweeney's overtime goal lifted the Cataracts to a 6-4 decision in game two. Playing-coach Don Howse (a Grand Falls native who enjoyed an outstanding professional career in the American Hockey League with the Montreal Canadiens' organization) and Wayne Dove each scored twice for the losers. Charlie Greene scored two goals keeping the Jets alive in the series with a 6-3 win. Terry Ryan's overtime marker gave Stephenville a 4-3 win in the fourth game to tie the series at two games apiece. But overtime goals by Bruce Campbell, his second of the game, and Tony Walsh earned the Cataracts a 6-4 decision to advance to the final.

Jeff Andrews' goal in the second overtime period powered Gander to their first win in the final, a 4-3 squeaker. Kirk Johnson, Gerry McCarron and Denis Laing also scored. Gene Faulkner had two goals for Grand Falls and Ron Sweeney added one. Goals by Laurie Cuvalier, Wayne Faulkner, Tony Cuomo and Tony Kennedy gave Grand Falls a 4-1 decision in the second game. Rick McCallum scored for Gander. Jeff Andrews sniped three goals, while Randy Pearcey and Darren Pickrem had two apiece, as Gander won the third game 10-4. Gerry McCarron, Zane Forbes and Rick McCallum added singles. Bruce Campbell, Gary Feener, Tony Grimes and Wayne Faulkner took care of the Grand Falls scoring. Steve Croucher netted the winner in overtime as Grand Falls tied the series with a 4-3 win. Gene Faulkner, Gary Feener and Tony Kennedy had the other tallies. Kirk Johnson, Terry Cooke and Darren Pickrem replied for the Flyers. Darren Pickrem netted two goals with singles coming from Jeff Andrews, Zane Forbes, Kirk Johnson, Rick McCallum and Terry Cooke as the Flyers edged into the series lead with a 7-4 victory in game five. Bill Laughery, Keith Boone, Wayne Faulkner and Steve Croucher scored for Grand Falls. Steve Croucher and Tony Cuomo each had two goals as Grand Falls tied the series with a 4-1 victory. Zane Forbes had the lone Gander goal. Laurie Cuvalier, Tony Walsh and Gary Feener scored the goals as Grand Falls won the Herder with a thrilling 3-2 decision. Darren Pickrem and Randy Pearcey were the Gander marksmen.

Grand Falls hosted the Thunder Bay Twins in the opening round of Allan Cup play. Despite two goals from Ron Sweeney and singles by Tony Cuomo, Terry Ryan and Steve Croucher, the Cataracts lost the opening game of the best-of-five series 6-5 in overtime. Ron Sweeney netted two more goals, while Tony Cuomo, Tom Coolen, Gary Feener and Terry Ryan chipped in with singles as the Cataracts defeated the Twins 7-4 in the second game. Tony Kennedy and Tony Walsh had a pair each and Steve Croucher had one as Grand Falls won game three 5-2. The Twins rebounded to tie the series with a 4-1 victory. But nothing could hold the Grand Falls team down, and with a fifth game 3-1 victory, the Grand Falls Cataracts became the first team in Newfoundland to defeat an Ontario senior-devision team in an Allan Cup series. Gene Faulkner, Terry Ryan and Laurie Cuvalier scored for the Cataracts. The team travelled to Sarnia, Ontario to meet the Petrolia Squires, but lost three straight to the Allan Cup champions by scores of 6-1, 6-3 and 8-0.

1983

With only four teams battling for the Herder Trophy in 1983, it was Stephenville's turn to stock up on players The Jets picked up Darren Pickrem from Gander, Terry Gillam, Bill Perry and Craig Scott from Corner Brook, lured Bruce Campbell away from Grand Falls and added imports Paul McInnis, Steve Robson, Jim Cahoon and Kevin Morrison to win its first Evening Telegram Trophy with 51 points. Grand Falls was second with 40 points, St. John's Capitals had 33 and the Shamrocks finished fourth with 27. Bruce Campbell captured his second straight scoring title with 73 points, while teammate Juan Strickland was second with 65. Zane Forbes of St. John's was third with 62 points, teammate Kirk Johnson had 59, the same as Paul McInnis of the Jets. The Capitals' goaltender Roger Kennedy was named the league's most valuable player. Juan Strickland, a native of Isle aux Morts who had an outstanding career with Acadia University in Atlantic college competition, was the rookie of the year and the winner of the Howie Clouter award. Stephenville goaltender Gary Dunville was the top netminder with a 3.33 average.

Juan Strickland

The Capitals surprised the Cataracts in the semi-final opener 5-4 as Erik Seaward, Zane Forbes, Terry Head, Glen Critch and Kirk Johnson scored the goals. Ron Sweeney netted two for Grand Falls and Tony

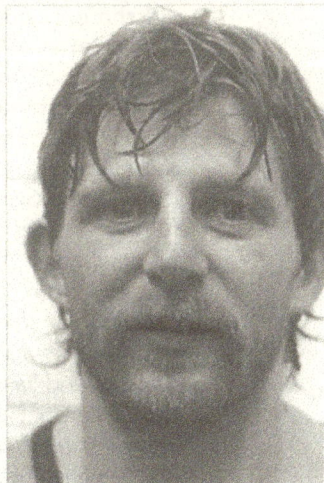

Cuomo and Gene Faulkner had one each. Former Washington Capitals star Tony White scored twice to lead Grand Falls to a 5-3 win in the second game. Other markers came from Gilbert Longpre, Keith Boone and Tony Grimes. Kirk Johnson had two and Glen Critch one for the Capitals. Goals by Randy Pearcey, Kirk Johnson and Glen Critch, together with Roger Kennedy's 31-save performance earned the Capitals a 3-0 shutout in the third contest. Grand Falls fought back to tie the series with a 4-1 victory as Tony Kennedy, Gilles Crepeau, Wayne Faulkner and Tony Cuomo scored. Zane Forbes had the only goal for the losers. Tony White, Gilles Crepeau and Tony Cuomo had goals for Grand Falls for a 3-2 win in the fifth and deciding contest to advance to the final. Glen Critch and Kirk Johnson scored for the Capitals. The Stephenville Jets required the minimum three games to eliminate the Shamrocks in their semi-final and earn their first-ever berth in the Herder final. Bruce Campbell had two goals in an opening-game 6-1 decision and Darren Pickrem's overtime marker gave the Jets a 5-4 victory in game two. Bruce Campbell and Darren Pickrem had two goals each in the 7-3 clincher.

Two goals by Gilles Crepeau and an outstanding 40-save performance by goaltender Dave Matte lifted the Cataracts to a 2-1 victory over Stephenville to open the finals. Paul McInnis had the only goal for the Jets who took control of the series with victories in each of the next three games. Darren Pickrem had two goals in a 5-3 victory during game two. Singles came from Don Howse, Charlie Greene and Kevin Morrison, while Terry Cooke, Greg Byrne and Gene Faulkner scored for the losers. Bruce Campbell had two goals, while Cal Dunville, Craig Scott, Terry Gillam and Wayne Dove had one apiece. Tony Cuomo was the only scorer for Grand Falls. With regular net-minder Gary Dunville on the injury list, the Jets picked up Roger Kennedy from St. John's. Kennedy promptly paid dividends, stopping 22 shots to give Stephenville a 3-0 victory in game four. Cal Dunville, Paul McInnis and Bruce Campbell scored the goals. Grand Falls remained alive in the series with a 5-2 win as Ron Sweeney, Gene Faulkner, Tony White, Greg Byrne and Tony Grimes scored. Bruce Campbell and Terry Gillam replied for Stephenville. Grand Falls tied the series with a 6-3 decision in game six. Terry Cooke, Ron Sweeney, Tony White, Greg Byrne, Wayne Faulkner and Tony Cuomo scored for the winners, while the losers had goals from Darren Pickrem, Steve Robson and Paul McInnis. Game seven was a titanic struggle, but the Jets prevailed for their first Herder with a 4-2 victory. Darren Pickrem led the way with a pair of goals, while singles came from Jim Cahoon and Juan Strickland. Ron Sweeney and Greg Byrne scored for Grand Falls.

The Allan Cup series with the Cambridge Hornets of Ontario was called the "overtime series" as three of the five games went into two extra periods. The Ontario club opened the series with a 4-3 victory in double overtime. Cal Dunville, Tony White and Zane Forbes scored for the Jets. Cambridge defeated Stephenville 5-2 in the second game with Juan Strickland and Zane Forbes scoring for the losing Jets. Darren Pickrem's overtime goal gave the Jets their first win in the series, a 3-2 victory, with Bruce Campbell and Juan Strickland also scoring in the game. Cal Dunville's goal in overtime made the difference as Stephenville tied the series with a 5-4 win in game four. Gordie Gallant had two for the Jets, with singles coming from Paul McInnis and Jim Cahoon. In the fifth and deciding game, three goals in the third period proved to be too much for the Jets as they lost 3-0.

1984

The Stephenville Jets won the Evening Telegram Trophy for their first-place finish in the 1983-84 season with 44 points, six more than the rebuilding Corner Brook Royals. The St. John's Capitals and Mike's Shamrocks combined as the Shamrock-Capitals to finish third with 35 points. The Port aux Basques Mariners made their debut into the senior loop and ended up with 22 points. Stephenville goaltender Gary Dunville was the league's top goaltender with a 3.64 mark. He was also named the most valuable player for the season and claimed the Gus Soper Memorial Trophy. Juan Strickland of Port aux Basques captured the scoring title with 92 points from 31 goals and 61 assists. Newcomer Tim Cranston of the Royals was second with 91 points, while Jeff Linesman of Port aux Basques had a league-leading 39 goals and 82 points. Tony White of Corner Brook also had 82 points and Sheldon Currie of Stephenville had 74. Corner Brook goaltender Rob Brown was named rookie of the year and Wayne Dove of Stephenville received the Howie Clouter award with 32 goals and 54 points for the season.

Darren Pickrem scored three goals, Sheldon Currie and Wayne Dove added two apiece, while playing-coach Don Howse had a goal and four assists to lead Stephenville to a 10-

2 triumph over Port aux Basques in the opening game of the semi-final. Wayne Dove contributed five goals, Darren Pickrem netted three and Cal Dunville and Kirk Johnson added a pair apiece as the Jets won the second game 16-2. They wrapped up the series with a 6-2 victory in game three as Darren Pickrem scored two more goals.

St. John's Shamrock-Capitals opened the other semi-final with a 7-5 victory over Corner Brook, but the Royals won the next three games to advance to the final. Two goals by Tony White paced the Royals to a 5-2 victory in game two, while Tony Cuomo's pair lifted Corner Brook to a 7-6 win in the third game. Tim Cranston netted a pair as the Royals eliminated the Capitals with a 4-1 decision.

Darren Pickrem and Sheldon Currie fired two goals apiece and singles came from Don Howse, Kirk Johnson and Cal Dunville as the Jets opened the Herder final with a 7-6 victory over the Royals. Craig Kennedy led the Royals with two markers and single tallies came off the sticks of Ron Sweeney, Tim Cranston, Doug King and Tony Cuomo. Wayne Dove's second goal of the game in overtime gave the Jets a 5-4 win in game two. Sheldon Currie, Darren Pickrem and Kirk Johnson also scored. Kev Lundrigan, Danny Cuomo, Tony White and Tim Cranston replied for Corner Brook. Stephenville raced to a 3-0 lead in the series with a 5-3 victory on goals by Cal Dunville, Steve McKenzie, Kirk Johnson, Don Howse and Zane Forbes. The Royals enjoyed goals from Terry Gillam, Doug King and Byron Rideout. Two-goal efforts by Jeff Regular and Danny Cuomo kept the Royals alive with a 10-3 win. Other goal scorers included Steve Dunne, Craig Scott, Ed Kearsey, Tim Cranston, Tony Cuomo and Doug King. Ken Bruce, Wayne Faulkner and Darren Pickrem scored for the Jets who wrapped up the Herder with a 6-1 victory in game five. Kirk Johnson led the winners with three goals, while singles came from Ken Bruce, Zane Forbes and Cal Dunville. Danny Cuomo had the lone Corner Brook tally.

The Jets travelled to Cambridge for a rematch in their Allan Cup series with the Ontario champions, but managed only one victory. The Hornets opened the series with an 8-5 decision and won the second game 7-5 in overtime. Kirk Johnson netted three goals, including the overtime winner, as Stephenville won game three 5-4, but fell 3-1 in the final contest.

1985

The 1985 edition of the Herder Memorial Trophy chase saw all four senior clubs load their rosters with import players as they attempted to claim the Herder Trophy and a crack at the Allan Cup. Stephenville repeated as first-place finishers with 58 points, while Corner Brook followed with 43. Port aux Basques jumped to third place with 28 points and Grand Falls finished in the basement with 15. Juan Strickland of Port aux Basques claimed his second straight scoring title with 88 points, edging Bruce Campbell of Stephenville who had 86. Zane Forbes of the Jets was named the league's most valuable player for the second time as he tallied 63 points during the regular season. Gary Dunville of Stephenville won his third straight goaltending award with a 3.52 average, while Andy Sullivan of the Jets was the Howie Clouter award winner. Corner Brook goaltender Kevin McCarthy was named rookie of the year with 12 victories and a 4.28 goals against average.

Bruce Campbell notched four goals and two assists, Cal Dunville had three goals and three helpers and Zane Forbes chipped in with two goals as Stephenville opened defence of the Herder with a 13-1 semi-final victory over Port aux Basques. Zane Forbes had two goals in the second game, a 9-6 decision. Gus Greco and Sheldon Currie had two apiece for the Mariners. Wayne Dove and Zane Forbes tallied twice apiece as Stephenville swept the series with a 9-5 win.

In the other series, two-goal performances by Whitney Richardson, Tony White and Tony Cuomo paced Corner Brook to an 8-3 victory over Grand Falls despite two goals from Cataract forward Richard Linteau. Tony White and Brad Fisher each connected twice as the Royals took the second game 12-3. Doug King found the range twice as Corner Brook advanced to the final with a 6-3 win.

Whitney Richardson and Tony Cuomo scored two goals apiece to lead the Royals to a 6-4 victory in the opening game of the final. Doug King and Steve Dunne added one each. Cal Dunville, Zane Forbes, Kevin Morrison and John Cossar scored for

Cal Dunville

113

Tony Cuomo

Stephenville. Goals by Bruce Campbell, Kevin Morrison, John White, Cal Dunville and Wade Fitzpatrick earned Stephenville a 5-4 victory in the second game. The Royals scored with goals from Tony Cuomo, Tony White, Doug King and Kirk Johnson. Talented winger Danny Cormier netted a pair of goals as the Royals took the series lead with a 5-1 victory. Doug King, Stan Hennigar and Kirk Johnson chipped in with singles. John Cossar had the lone Stephenville marker. Rugged defenceman Jeff Leverman and Bruce Campbell had two markers apiece and Paul Reid added a single as the Jets tied the series with a 5-3 win. Bob O'Neill, Kirk Johnson and Tony Cuomo replied for the Royals. Goals by Tony Cuomo, Stan Hennigar and Kirk Johnson earned Corner Brook a 3-2 victory in game five. John White and Randy Pearcey netted the Stephenville goals. Ray Baird and Tony White had two goals each and singles came from Terry Gillam, Bob O'Neill and Steve Dunne as Corner Brook captured its first Herder since 1977 with a 7-2 decision. Andy Sullivan and John White scored for the Jets.

The Royals gave the province its first real run at the Allan Cup as they opened against the Riverview Trappers from New Brunswick. Jeff Leverman, added from the Jets, had a goal and two assists in an opening game 4-2 victory for the Royals, while Tony White scored twice and assisted on three more goals that gave Corner Brook a 7-4 decision in game two. The Royals eliminated the Maritime champions 12-4 in the deciding game with Doug King, Zane Forbes, Cal Dunville and Steve Dunne each scoring twice.

Ontario's Hamilton-Dundas Hawks were the next team to visit Humber Gardens in Corner Brook, but fared no better than the Trappers. Tony Cuomo's second goal of the game in overtime gave the Royals a 9-8 victory in the opening game. Bruce Campbell netted four goals and Cal Dunville added a goal and three assists to give the Royals a 10-2 decision in the second contest. Doug King, Dan Cormier and Tony Cuomo had two goals apiece as Corner Brook raced to a 3-0 lead in the best-of-seven series with a 6-4 win. They clinched the G. P. Bolton Trophy for the first time and a berth in the eastern Allan Cup

114

final with a 6-5 victory when Bob O'Neill and Zane Forbes each fired two goals in game four.

The powerful Thunder Bay Twins were the next opponents for the Royals. The Corner Brook team kept their winning streak alive with a 9-5 victory in game one. Doug King and Bruce Campbell each scored twice for the winners. In game two, Goaltender Dave Matte kicked out 33 shots, while Cal Dunville, Tony Cuomo and Tony White connected in overtime for a 3-0 win. Another 9-5 victory in game three, with Tony Cuomo and Cal Dunville each potting a pair of tallies, put the Royals to within one game of a berth in the Allan Cup final. But then the Cinderella season came to an end. Internal bickering among the players left the team less than prepared for game four, enabling the Twins to stay alive for a 4-2 win. Things were no better in game five and the Twins thumped the Royals 8-3. Thunder Bay tied the series with a 2-0 shutout in game six, and advanced to the final by stunning the Royals 5-4 in game seven to complete the amazing four-game comeback.

1986

Stephenville and Corner Brook continued their tight battle for the 1986 Herder with both teams battling on even terms for most of the season. The Jets were trying to reclaim the Herder, while the Royals wanted another crack at the Allan Cup that eluded their grasp the previous year. The league was reduced to just three teams when Grand Falls decided not to enter and Port aux Basques pulled out in January after winning just two of 22 games. The Jets became the first team to win the Evening Telegram Trophy four times in a row with 65 points, while Corner Brook had 52 and St. John's 20. In the three-team round robin semi-final series, Stephenville again came out on top with 11 wins for 22 points, Corner Brook gained the other berth in the final with 18 points, while the Capitals managed only eight. Corner Brook goaltender Dave Matte was named the regular season most valu-

Robbie Forbes

able player after winning the goaltender award with a 3.75 average and posting 18 wins during the season. Andy Sullivan

of Stephenville won his second straight Howie Clouter award, while the scoring title went to newcomer Robbie Forbes of Corner Brook who had 117 points on 53 goals and 64 assists. Andy Sullivan was next with 96 points, while Royals' Dan Cormier had 80. Sheldon Currie of Stephenville and Richard Linteau of St. John's had 78 points apiece. The top rookie was Corner Brook's Ken Mercer with 47 points.

Forward Sheldon Currie and defenceman Steve McKenzie each potted a pair of goals as Stephenville drew first blood in the Herder final with a 7-3 decision over the Royals. Andy Sullivan, Mike Jeffrey and Dave Stoyanovich chipped in with singles. Ken Mercer, Todd Stark and Stan Hennigar replied for the losers. A goal by Robbie Forbes in the second overtime period gave the Royals a 7-6 victory to even the series. Todd Stark led the winners with three goals and two assists, while singles came from Dan Cormier, Byron Rideout and Tim Cranston. Mike Jeffrey, Bruce Rugelis, Paul Jeffrey, Kevin Morrison, Cal Dunville and Steve McKenzie replied in a losing cause. Robbie Forbes tallied three times as the Royals took the series lead with an 8-4 win. Darryl Ulrich, Tim Cranston, Steve Gallant, Tony Cuomo and Dan Cormier also had goals. Dave Stoyanovich, Mike Jeffrey and Andy Sullivan, the only Newfoundlander to get a goal in the game, replied for the Jets. Corner Brook took a stranglehold on the Herder final with a 6-5 win in game four as Tim Cranston fired a pair. Other goals came from Mac Tucker, Ken Mercer, Dan Cormier and Gilbert Longpre. Mike Jeffrey, Andy Sullivan, Steve McKenzie and Dave Stoyanovich scored the Stephenville markers. The Jets stayed alive in the series with a 5-3 victory on goals by Bruce Rugelis, Sheldon Currie, Mike Jeffrey, Dave Stoyanovich and Cal Dunville. Mark Jeffries, Stan Hennigar and Robbie Forbes had the goals for the Royals. Corner Brook won the Herder with a 7-4 decision in game six when Robbie Forbes scored three times and Todd Stark added a goal and three assists. Ed Kearsey, Ken Mercer and Tim Cranston also scored. The Jets got goals from Mike Jeffrey, Bruce Rugelis, Kevin Morrison and Zane Forbes.

The Royals began their quest for the historic Allan Cup with a trip to Brantford, Ontario, to take on the Flamboro Mott's Clamatos in the eastern final. Tim Cranston poked in two goals and Todd Stark added three assists as the Royals won the opening game by a 5-2 count. Tim Cranston had two more in a 7-4 loss in game two. Dan Cormier and Robbie Forbes scored the only Corner Brook goals in a 6-2 loss in game three. The Royals came back the next night to tie the series with another 5-2 win as Robbie Forbes and Steve McKenzie each netted a pair of markers and Tim Cranston fired his fifth of the series. The Royals were trounced 11-5 in the fifth game with Dan Cormier scoring twice. With their backs against the wall, the Royals came out storming in game six and skated off with an 8-4 victory as Gus Greco notched two goals and two assists and Ed Kearsey assisted three times. The Royals grabbed a 3-0 lead in the first period of game seven and never looked back as they stopped the Clamatos 8-5 for their second straight win on the Bolton Trophy. Tim Cranston, playing with a broken wrist, Gus Greco and Dan Cormier each scored twice for the Corner Brook squad. Cal Dunville had a goal and three assists, while Robbie Forbes scored the other goal.

The Allan Cup final in Nelson, British Columbia, was the next test for the Royals and they handled the challenge well. Two-goal performances by Steve McKenzie and Tim Cranston paved the way to a 6-4 victory for the Royals in the opening game. A goal by Robbie Forbes midway through the third period stood up as the winner in a 6-5 triumph during the rough second game that saw more than 200 minutes in penalties being assessed. Todd Stark pulled the trigger on four goals during the third game, leading the Royals to a 5-2 victory. Determined not to make the same mistake as the year before when they let a 3-0 lead in the series slip away, the Royals stormed to the attack in the fourth game and humbled the host team 7-0 with series most valuable player Dave Matte stopping 34 shots for the shutout. Sheldon Currie had two goals and three assists, while Tony Cuomo and Ed Kearsey each added two goals and Tim Cranston completed the scoring.

The Royals added another first to their impressive list with their victory in the series. In addition to being the first Herder Memorial Trophy champions in 1935 and Eastern Canadian and E. P. Bolton Trophy winners in 1985, they now become the first Newfoundland team to win the prestigious Allan Cup. One of the biggest motorcades ever seen on the west coast greeted the Royals upon their arrival at Stephenville air-

Dave Matte

117

port. It measured about five miles in length and escorted the Royals through the streets of Corner Brook before culminating with victory celebrations at Humber Gardens.

Cliff Gorman was president of the Corner Brook Hockey Association during this monumental season and Mike Anderson was head coach. Former player Terry Gillam was his assistant. The players included captain Craig Kennedy, goalies Dave Matte, Dan Longe, Kevin McCarthy and Gerry Barry, defencemen Ed Kearsey, Darryl Ulrich, Gilbert Longpre, Steve McKenzie, Kevin Lundrigan, Ray Baird, Steve Gallant, Bill Breen, Bob O'Neill and Stan Hennigar, along with forwards Dan Cormier, Robbie Forbes, Sheldon Currie, Cal Dunville, Tony Cuomo, Ken Mercer, Todd Stark, Gus Greco, Byron Rideout, Don Bennett, Mac Tucker and Tim Cranston.

1987

The St. John's Capitals took their turn at trying to buy into the Herder by opening their purse strings and adding several players for the 1987 Herder playoffs. Likeable Bill Riley, a former professional with the Washington Capitals, was brought in as playing-coach. The Caps also added Gus Greco, Bob O'Neill and Mac Tucker from Corner Brook, picked up Andy Sullivan from Stephenville and signed former pros Russ Adam, John Hutchings and Hilton Ruggles. The Capitals easily captured first place and the Evening Telegram Trophy with their 70 points, while Stephenville placed second with 53. Corner Brook managed 44 points and Mount Pearl, the league's newest entry, picked up nine points in fourth place.

The Grand Falls Cataracts were set to return to the senior loop after a year's absence, but, according to then-general manager Bob Molloy it was just too costly a proposition. "We felt it would take at least $250,000 to ice a competitive team and we wanted no part of that. At that time, we had $8,000 in the bank and we distributed the money to various charities in the Grand Falls area," he disclosed.

Andy Sullivan established a league-record with 86 assists and tallied 44 goals to walk away with the scoring title with 130 points. For his efforts, he was also named the league's most valuable player. Corner Brook's Robbie Forbes was second in the scoring race with 127 points, including 60 goals, and picked up the Howie Clouter award. Dan Cormier of the Royals was third with 108 points, while Hilton Ruggles of the Capitals and Jack MacKeigan of Stephenville each had 105. The Capitals' goaltender Peter White was named rookie of the year after leading all goaltenders with a 3.39 goals against average.

Bill Riley paced the way with three goals, while Gerry Nottall and Russ Adam each contributed a pair as the Capitals opened the semi-finals with a 10-5 victory over Mount Pearl. Andy Sullivan notched a hat-trick in game two as the Capitals took a 9-5 decision. The St. John's team completely dominated the third game and won the series with a 17-4 win as Bill Riley netted six goals and helped on three more. Andy Sullivan and Gus Greco each had two goals and five assists, while Bill Walsh chipped in with a pair.

Bill Riley

Two-goal performances from former Toronto Maple Leaf Gary Yaremchuk paced Corner Brook to 7-2 and 5-2 victories over Stephenville as the other semi-final opened on the west coast. But the Jets stayed alive in game three with a 2-1 win as Dave McQueen tallied the winner in the third period. Jack MacKeigan's three goals helped Stephenville tie the series with a 6-5 victory. Robbie Forbes and Sheldon Currie had two-goal efforts for the Royals. Stephenville completed the comeback with a 6-2 win to take the series three games to two as Bruce Rugelis netted two goals and Jack MacKeigan sniped one and assisted on two more. Dan Cormier had both Corner Brook markers.

St. John's dominated the opening game of the final by posting an 8-1 victory over Stephenville as Andy Sullivan had two goals and four assists. The other markers came off the sticks of Russ Adam, Bob O'Neill, Hilton Ruggles, Bill Riley, Mac Tucker and Gus Greco. Jack MacKeigan replied for the losers. Goals by Bill Riley, Richard Linteau, Hilton Ruggles, Andy Sullivan and Bill Walsh paced St. John's to a 5-3 win in game two. Dave McQueen, Bob Lambe and Juan Strickland replied for the Jets. Stephenville fell behind three games to none in losing game three 4-1 as Andy Sullivan, Gus Greco, John Hutchings and Russ Adam netted the goals. Steve McKenzie had the Stephenville marker. The Jets stayed alive in the series by winning game four 6-5 as Dave McQueen and Steve McKenzie each scored twice. Steve Schrumph and Kevin Morrison had singles. Richard Linteau, Russ Adam, Zane Forbes, Gus Greco and Andy Sullivan scored in a losing cause. A 5-2 victory earned the Jets their second win in the series with Steve McKenzie potting a pair of markers. Singles came from Bruce Rugelis, Don Howse and Cal Dunville. Hilton Ruggles and Russ Adam scored for the Capitals. St. John's rallied for a 12-6 win in the sixth game to clinch the Herder. Bill Riley paced the winners with four goals, while Russ Adam had two goals and two assists and Hilton Ruggles notched one goal and assisted on four more. Bruce Rugelis led the Jets with four goals and Dave McQueen chipped in with the other two.

The Capitals opened the eastern Allan Cup playoffs at Memorial Stadium against the Charlottetown Islanders and took the series three games to one. Two-goal performances from Russ Adam and John Hutchings led the winners to a 9-1 victory in game one. John Hutchings added two goals in game two, but the Islanders prevailed by a 4-3 score. Andy Sullivan and Gus Greco each had two goals and Dave Matte kicked out 31 shots as St. John's rolled to a 7-0 win in the third game. Bill Riley's pair led the Capitals to the next round with a 3-2 win in the fourth contest. The Caps took on the Brantford Mott's Clamatos in the eastern final, but came out on the short end of a 4-2 score in the best-of-seven series. Hilton Ruggles and Russ Adam each had two goals in a 6-4 win and the club got goals from five different players to win the third game 5-2. Brantford won the final three games of the series, including the clincher, 3-2 in double overtime.

1988

The 1987-88 Newfoundland senior hockey season drew six entries, although the performance of the Gander Internationals didn't endear them to hockey fans throughout the province. The Gander club won only one of 48 games and opposing players feasted on the hapless club to establish several scoring marks. Craig Jenkins, a native of Prince Edward Island, signed by the Corner Brook Royals, established new scoring records for total points and assists with 55 goals and 102 assists for a total of 157 points. Bill MacDougall of St. John's finished second with 137 points from 66 goals and 71 assists. Michel Couvrette of Stephenville set the all-time goal-scoring mark with 68 tallies and added 66 assists for 134 points. Richard Linteau of Mount

Pearl also broke the 60-goal mark with 65 and tallied 57 assists for 122 points. Andy Sullivan of St. John's and Todd Stark of Corner Brook each had 117 points and Brad Fisher of the Caps followed with 115 points. Craig Jenkins was also named winner of the Howie Clouter award, while Dan Cormier of Corner Brook was voted the most valuable player with 103 points. Gander's Derek Dalley was rookie of the year with 28 goals and 33 assists for 61 points and Roger Kennedy of the Capitals led all goaltenders with a 3.85 average and two shutouts.

Craig Jenkins continued his torrid scoring in the playoffs with three goals in game one as the Royals opened the semifinal series with a 7-4 victory over Stephenville. Ali Butorac chipped in with a pair of markers, while Gilbert Longpre and Cal Dunville each had two for Stephenville. The Jets evened the series with a 7-3 victory in game two with Sheldon Currie and Jack MacKeigan each scoring twice. The Royals had two goals from Jeff Regular and a goal and three assists from Robbie Forbes to stop the Jets 8-2 for a game three decision. Tim Brantner and Sheldon Currie had two markers apiece as the Jets tied the series with a 6-4 victory. The Jets went ahead by stopping the Royals 6-2 in game five. Sheldon Currie paced the winners with three goals. Robbie Forbes, Darren McWhirter, Mark Zeitlin and Todd Stark scored the goals that led the Royals to a 4-1 decision in game six. The Jets were eliminated with a 5-3 loss in the seventh game on two-goal performances from Dan Cormier and Robbie Forbes. Craig Jenkins had the other goal. Michel Couvrette had two and Jack MacKeigan one for Stephenville.

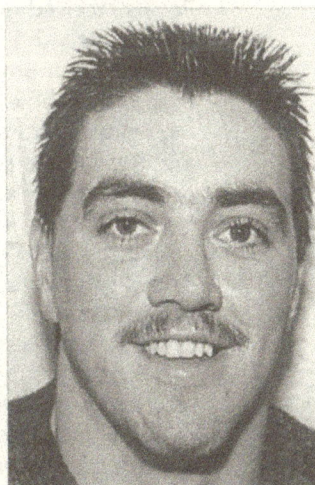

Dan Cormier

Andy Sullivan's two goals paced the Capitals, the first-place finishers, to an opening 5-1 playoff victory over the Port aux Basques Mariners. However, the Mariners fought back to take game two 7-4 with Ron Chyzowski and Joe West scoring two goals each and Juan Strickland adding a goal and three helpers. Zane Forbes had two for the Capitals. Steve Scott and Zane Forbes each had two as the Caps won game three 5-4. Joe West replied twice for the Mariners. Bill Riley scored three times and Zane Forbes added a pair to give the Caps a 7-6 decision in the fourth game with Ron Chyzowski and Rene Lecuyer each hav-

121

ing a pair for the losers. The Caps edged the Mariners 4-3 in game five to advance to the final. Joe West had two goals in a losing cause.

Dan Cormier scored three times and set up two goals by Robbie Forbes to lead Corner Brook to a 9-5 win over the Capitals in the opening game of the 1988 Herder final. The Royals also got goals from Chip Crandell, Jeff Andrews, Todd Stark and Darren McWhirter. Zane Forbes had two for the Caps and Steve Scott, Brad Fisher and Ed Oates added singles. The Capitals rebounded in the second game to tie the series with a 9-4 decision. Bill MacDougall netted three for the winners, Zane Forbes two and Andy Sullivan, who also had four assists counted for two more. Russ Adam and Bill Riley chipped in with singles. Dan Cormier and Ed Kearsey each scored twice for the Royals. With all the scoring coming in the first period, the Royals received goals from Todd Stark and Dan Cormier to nip the Capitals 2-1 in game three. Russ Adam replied for the losers. Corner Brook took a big lead with a 5-3 victory in game four with Robbie Forbes notching a hat-trick and singles coming from Todd Stark and Marc Zeitlin. Zane Forbes, Brad Fisher and Russ Adam scored for the Capitals. Dan Cormier's second goal of the game in overtime lifted the Royals to another Herder with a 4-3 decision. Ed Kearsey and Robbie Forbes added the other goals, while Zane Forbes, Bill MacDougall and Andy Sullivan replied for the Capitals. Dan Cormier led all playoff scorers with 24 points, while Robbie Forbes had 21 and Andy Sullivan was third with 18.

For the first time since 1967, the branch did not send a representative to the Allan Cup competition. Although it wasn't realized then, Newfoundland's love affair with the Allan Cup was officially over. Except for a run at the Hardy Cup the following year, Newfoundland senior clubs would not enter senior playoffs with mainland teams again.

1989

The storied Newfoundland senior hockey league had its final year of competition as a province-wide league in 1988-89 with four teams battling for the Herder Memorial Trophy. The season proved to be very competitive as the St. John's Capitals claimed the Evening Telegram Trophy with 45 points, followed closely by Port aux Basques, Corner Brook and Stephenville. Both semi-final playoffs produced some of the finest hockey played in many years as St. John's tangled with Stephenville and Corner Brook played off with Port aux Basques. Mariners' defenceman Marc West was voted the most valuable player for the season, leading all defencemen with 34 goals and 43 assists for 77 points. His goal total fell one short of the mark established by George Faulkner in 1966-67. The Capitals' Andy Sullivan won the scoring title with 106 points, while Len Soccio of Port aux Basques was second with 88 points. Tim Ferguson of Stephenville tied Marc West with 77 points and Juan Strickland of the Mariners was next with 74. Roger Kennedy of St. John's captured his third goaltending crown with a 4.28 goals against average and Brent Jenkins of the Royals was named rookie of the year. Darren McWhirter of Corner Brook claimed the Howie Clouter award.

Two goals by Russ Adam and one by Andy Sullivan paced St. John's to a 3-1 win over Stephenville to open the semi-finals. Ron McLean replied for the Jets. The Capitals had two goals from Gerry Noftall to hammer Stephenville 8-2 in the second game. The Jets were back in the series on home ice as Wayne Dove and Cal Dunville fired two goals each, leading Stephenville to a 6-5 triumph. Zane Forbes netted two for the Capitals. Three goals by Cal Dunville and two goals and three helpers by John Hanna powered the Jets to an 8-2 victory in game four to tie the series. Brad Fisher had two goals, Bill Riley added the winner and Andy Sullivan set up all three tallies as the Capitals took the series lead with a 3-2 decision. Chris Hoyles and John Hanna had the Stephenville goals. John Hutchings' goal in overtime lifted the Caps to a 3-2 victory in the sixth game to advance to the final. Paul Shears and Bill Riley also scored for the Caps, while Chris Hoyles and Jack MacKeigan replied for Stephenville.

Juan Strickland's two goals enabled the Mariners to open the other semi-final with a 7-3 decision over the Royals. But the Corner Brook squad had two goals from Todd Stark and a goal and two assists from Dan Cormier to tie the series with a 7-5 victory. Juan Strickland and Bill MacDougall each netted two goals, giving the Mariners a 6-5 win in the third game as Dan Cormier had two for the losers. Tim Cranston powered the Royals to the tie in the series with two goals in an 8-3 triumph in game four. Dave McLay scored twice for the Mariners. Port aux Basques forged ahead in the series with a 6-3 victory in game five as Bill MacDougall had two goals and Marc West added four assists. Ed Kearsey had two of the three Corner Brook goals. Ed Kearsey notched two goals and two assists and Dan Cormier chipped in with a goal and two assists as Corner Brook tied the series with a 6-1 victory, setting the stage for the seventh contest at the Bruce Arena in Port aux Basques. Bill MacDougall fired two goals and Joe West and Don Howse had one each as the Mariners advanced to their first ever Herder final with a 4-1 victory. Don McGrath replied for the Royals.

The Herder final opened in St. John's and the Mariners surprised the Capitals 4-3 on Marc West's overtime goal. Juan Strickland led the way with two goals and John Witzke added one. John Hutchings, Andy Sullivan and Gerry Noftall scored in a losing cause. Andy Sullivan, who also had three assists, Bill Riley and Gerry Noftall each scored twice as the Caps battled back for a 6-3 decision. Marc and Joe West and Don Howse had the goals for Port aux Basques. The Capitals took a 2-1 lead when they upended the Mariners 7-2 in game three. Brad Fisher and Zane Forbes each had two goals, while singles came from Andy Sullivan, Gerry Noftall and Tony Cuomo. Andy Sullivan also chipped in with three assists. Don Howse and Bill MacDougall scored for the Mariners.

The atmosphere was electrifying in tiny Bruce Arena as more than 2,000 screaming fans awaited the Mariners and Capitals for game four. With the sounds of train horns and chanting fans to urge them on, the Mariners tied the series with an 8-4 decision as Len Soccio and Bill MacDougall each scored twice. Singles came from Brian Burley, Dwayne Joyce, Dave McLay and Joe West. Russ Adam had two for the Caps who got one apiece from Brad Fisher and Andy Sullivan. Chris Pusey stopped 35 shots and Marc West netted a pair of goals as the Mariners blanked the Capitals 6-0 in game five. Len Soccio, Dwayne Joyce, Bill MacDougall and Don Howse added singles. The Mariners claimed their first Herder Trophy with a 2-1 victory in the sixth game on goals by Juan Strickland and Bill MacDougall. Russ Adam replied for the Capitals.

The Mariners represented the province at the Canadian senior "B" hockey championships for the Hardy Cup. Bolstered by six players from the other senior clubs, the Mariners iced a potent lineup when they took on the Dartmouth Mounties from Nova Scotia and won the series three games to one. After losing the opening contest 8-2, the Mariners bounced back with 7-4, 8-3 and 6-4 decisions. Joe West was the leader in that series with four goals and three assists, while Don Howse and Juan Strickland each picked up six points.

The Mariners next hosted the Durham Huskies from Ontario in the battle for the Col. J. Bourque Cup. After winning the opening game 4-3 on Len Soccio's overtime goal, the Mariners were never pressed and stopped the Huskies 12-0 and 8-5 to clinch the eastern title. Dwayne Joyce had three goals in the second game, while Todd Savoury and Gus Greco had two each. Chris Pusey stopped 25 shots for the second game shutout, while Gus Greco and Todd Stark each scored twice in the third game.

The Kindersley, from Saskatchewan, travelled to Port aux Basques for the Hardy Cup final. Two-goal performances by Joe West, Todd Savoury and Juan Strickland, powered the Mariners to a 9-5 victory in the opening contest. Joe West and Dave McLay each registered two-goal efforts in the second game, leading the host club to a 10-5 win. Port aux Basques took a stranglehold on the series with a 6-5 win in the third game as Juan Strickland notched a pair of tallies. The Mariners eased up in the fourth game and dropped a 5-3 decision to the Saskatchewan club, but rebounded in game five for a 7-2 triumph and the first-ever Hardy Cup for Newfoundland. Len Soccio had two goals for the Mariners who had singles from Dave McLay, Juan Strickland, Marc West, Bill Riley and Brian Burley.

When the Newfoundland senior hockey clubs met for their annual fall meeting in September of 1989, the prospects for another hockey season didn't look bright. Only two clubs were interested, or had the financial capabilities, to ice a team for the 1990 Herder Memorial Trophy playoffs. With a debt approaching $200,000, the Stephenville Jets decided to pack it in. They were followed by the Port aux Basques Mariners who were in-the-red to the tune of $90,000. Although the Corner Brook Royals owed about $120,000, they were still interested in competing for another year, while the St. John's Capitals, who also owed more than $50,000, were also willing to play. However, with only two teams interested, the league officially decided to abandon play for the season.

Something for Everyone

where else but at the

SUNDANCE

Featuring a fine array of wines,
martinis and cigars.

Catering services, private functions
and meeting rooms available.

HAPPY HOUR
3–7 PM DAILY

Seafood and steakhouse on the premises.

CORNER OF GEORGE & ADELAIDE STREET
(709) 753-7822

CHAPTER 6

Back to the Local Level

In an effort to keep hockey interest alive on the east coast, a four-team senior league was initiated in the fall of 1989, but folded after only two games. Negotiations carried on for most of the winter in an effort to keep the senior league alive and an interim solution was reached during the spring of 1990. The St. John's Capitals would meet an all-star team from the Avalon East intermediate league in an eastern semi-final, with the winner advancing against the Bonavista Cabots, leaders of the central Beothuck league. Corner Brook and Stephenville, using local players, would play in the west, with the eventual winners meeting for the Herder Trophy.

Andy Sullivan netted a pair of goals and Zane Forbes, together with playing-coach Russ Adam, added one each as the Capitals stopped Avalon East 4-1 in their opening game. Tony Hawco replied for the losers. Zane Forbes and Andy Sullivan each netted two goals as the Capitals took the second game 6-5. Brad Fisher and Steve Joy also scored for the winners, while Ed Tapper led Avalon East with a goal and three assists. Other markers came from Tom Fitzpatrick, Bill Windsor, Doug Russell and John Goss. Andy Sullivan's two goals paced St. John's to a 4-3 victory in the third game to sweep the series. Peter Hanlon and Gerry Noftall also scored, while Derek Pelley, Tom Fitzpatrick and Doug Russell netted the Avalon East goals. Brad Fisher had four goals and Zane Forbes chipped in with three as the Capitals downed Bonavista 9-2 in the eastern final. Russ Adam scored twice and Brad Fisher added a goal and four helpers as the Capitals stopped the Cabots 10-4 to sweep the series.

Sean Reader pulled the trigger on five goals as Corner Brook took a 12-5 victory over Stephenville. Craig Jackson and Glen Allan chipped in with two goals each for the winners. Rob Abbott had two for the Jets. Brent Jenkins scored twice as the Royals won the second game 5-4. Peter Smith scored three times in a losing cause. Brent Jenkins, Craig Jackson and Ed

Kearsey had two goals apiece as Corner Brook won the third game 10-6 despite a three-goal performance by Craig Payne of the Jets. Sean Reader fired three goals and set up two more as Corner Brook advanced to the final with an 8-3 decision. Ben Lane fired two goals for the losers.

Zane Forbes tallied three times and Andy Sullivan scored in the second overtime period to give the Capitals a 6-5 win over Corner Brook in the opening game of the Herder final. Dave Bennett and Russ Adam also scored for the winners. Ed Kearsey netted two goals for the Royals. The Caps trounced Corner Brook 12-4 in the second game, with Brad Fisher scoring three times, Andy Sullivan adding a goal and four assists, and Ward Gosse, Peter Hanlon and Russ Adam adding two-goal each. Cal Dunville had a goal and two assists for the losers. Russ Adam and Ward Gosse fired two goals apiece and Andy Sullivan set up four tallies as St. John's doubled the Royals 6-3 in game three. Glen Allan had two Corner Brook markers. St. John's swept to the Herder victory with a 10-3 decision in game four as Russ Adam, Andy Sullivan and Ward Gosse led the winners with two goals apiece. Lloyd Locke had two tallies for the Royals.

Things didn't get any better for the senior clubs as plans were being made for the 1990-91 hockey season. Various club officials attempted to generate interest in re-establishing the league, but there wasn't enough interest to warrant a provincial operation

Pat Daly of the St. John's Capitals felt disappointed that the league was not able to keep going but said, "there's no way we can keep a team together all year to play off for the Herder at the end of the season. If we don't have a league, then I guess we're finished." And for the first time since 1942-43, the Herder Memorial Trophy was not awarded in 1991.

1992

The battle for the Herder came full circle in 1992, when it was decided that the winners of the two senior leagues in Newfoundland would play for the coveted trophy, much the same as had occurred back in that first season in 1935. The Flatrock Flyers of the Avalon East division and the Badger Bombers, champions of the central league, would meet in a best-of-five series to determine the Newfoundland senior hockey champion. Using only local players, the two tiny communities provided a spirited battle for the top senior hockey prize.

Goals by Wayne Little, Russ Kennedy, Keith Loder, Dave Jacobs and Craig Tulk lifted Badger to a 5-4 win to open the series. Terry Peddle, Ed Oates, Kirby Dumaresque and Tony Hawco replied for Flatrock. The Flyers battled back in the second game to take a 5-2 decision on goals by Ray Hefferman, Ed Oates, Robert Bradbury, Tony Hawco and Derek Pelley. Russ Kennedy and Steve Barnes were the Badger marksmen. The Bombers got a pair of goals from Greg Price to stop Flatrock 7-3 in the third contest. Singles came from Craig Tulk, Hubie Hollett, Bob Bugden, Russ Kennedy and George Penney. Jeff Sullivan, Robert Bradbury and Joey Maynard had the Flatrock goals. Russ Kennedy's third goal of the game in overtime earned the Bombers the Herder with a 5-4 victory over Flatrock. Barry Manuel and Greg Price also connected. Robert Bradbury, Tony Hawco, John Goss and Warren Sullivan replied for Flatrock.

1993

The Conception Bay South intermediate league decided to join the chase for the Herder in 1993, giving the senior division three champions from which to determine a provincial winner. Flatrock emerged as winners in Avalon East by defeating Pouch Cove four games to one, while Bell Island took care of Kelligrews by the same count in the Conception Bay league. Gander stopped Badger in five games to claim the central title.

Robert Bradbury, Lee Hawco, Kirby Dumaresque and Derek Pelley scored the goals as Flatrock edged Bell Island 4-3 to open their series. Chris Ford, Bill Williams and Wayne Bennett replied for the Islanders. Goals by Ed Oates, Robert Bradbury and Lee Hawco gave Flatrock a 3-2 win over Bell Island and the eastern championship. Wayne Bennett and Chris Ford scored for the losers.

Jack Kane's goal in overtime earned Flatrock a 3-2 victory over Gander in the opening game of the final. Ed Oates and Kirby Dumaresque added the other markers. Ken MacDonald and Jason Boyd scored for Gander. Ed Oates and Jack Kane had two-goal performances as Flatrock tripped Gander 8-3 in the second game. Tony and Lee Hawco, Robert Bradbury and Kirby Dumaresque also scored. Jamie Newman, Dennis Briffitt and Brent Jenkins had the Gander goals. The Gander club rebounded in game three with a 9-4 victory as Chris Conrad and Russ Gosse each scored twice. Singles came from Brent Jenkins, Ken MacDonald, Barry Hammond, Mel Best and Rick Sheppard. Kirby Dumaresque had two for Flatrock, while Jack Kane and Kevin Parsons sniped singles. Gander evened the series at two games apiece with a 6-4 victory in the fourth game. Chris Conrad and Brent Jenkins had two goals each and Rick Sheppard and Todd Baldwin added singles. Jack Kane led the eastern champions with two goals, while Kevin Parsons and Paul Shears had one each. Defenceman Derek Pelley pulled the trigger on three goals as Flatrock claimed its first Herder with a 7-4 win in the fifth and deciding contest. Tony Hawco, Jack Kane, Ed Oates and Jeff Sullivan chipped in with a goal each. Ken MacDonald, Jamie Newman, Todd Baldwin and Dennis Briffitt scored in a losing cause.

For the first time since the 1989-90 season, the NLHA re-instituted the provincial awards. Andy Sullivan, playing with Pouch Cove of the Avalon East league, claimed the scoring title with 63 points and was named the senior division's most valuable player. Bell Island of the Conception Bay South league was the Evening Telegram winner, while Roger Kennedy of Badger was the top goaltender with a 3.13 average. Teammate Russ Kennedy was the Howie Clouter winner and Bill Williams of Bell Island was named the top rookie.

1994

The formation of the Avalon West senior league, combined with solid leagues in the Avalon East and Central Newfoundland divisions resulted in strong competition during the 1994 Herder Memorial Trophy playoffs. Bill Bishop of Portugal Cove was named winner of the Gus Soper most valuable player award, while the Howie Clouter award went to Derek Dalley of LaScie. Andy Sullivan of Southern Shore captured his fourth provincial scoring title with 49 points, while Roger Kennedy of Badger won the top goaltending award in the province for the fifth time. Kevin Fitzpatrick of Torbay was named rookie of the year and the Southern Shore Breakers won the Evening Telegram Trophy for finishing first in the Avalon West league.

Southern Shore opened the best-of-three provincial semifinal with a 5-3 victory over Flatrock as Gary Furlong, Ward Gosse, Bill Windsor, Ken Dinn and Andy Sullivan scored the goals. Ed Oates, Joey Maynard and Robert Bradbury replied for Flatrock, who took the second game of the series 7-4, with Ed Oates counting twice. Singles came from Joey Maynard, Kirby Dumaresque, John Bolger, Warren Sullivan and Robert Bradbury. Andy and Gary Sullivan, Bill Windsor and Gary Furlong replied for the Breakers. The Southern Shore went on to take the series with a 3-2 victory in the deciding game on goals by Wayne Carew, Bill Windsor and Cory Frizzell. Ed Oates and Warren Sullivan scored for Flatrock.

Paced by the three-goal performance of Guy Gray, the LaScie Jets opened the Herder final with a 7-5 decision over Southern Shore. Derek Dalley chipped in with two goals andDoug Ward along with former

Roger Kennedy

Port aux Basques Mariner Juan Strickland added singles. Bill Windsor and Ward Gosse led the Breakers with two goals and Andy Sullivan added a single. The Jets opened a two-game lead with a 5-3 victory in the second game as Neil Ward, Craig Young, Derek Dalley, Dave Ward and Guy Gray scored the goals. Gary Furlong, Andy and Gary Sullivan scored for Southern Shore. The Breakers captured one game in the series when it resumed in Mobile with a 7-4 decision over the Jets. Gary Sullivan had three goals and two assists, Bill Windsor netted two goals and had five helpers, while Andy Sullivan scored the other two and set up four more. Mel Best, Derek Dalley, Rob Varrin and Clint Gaudon scored for LaScie. The Breakers tied the series with a 5-1 victory with Andy Sullivan accounting for two goals and two assists. Singles came from Bill Windsor, Gary Sullivan and Gary Furlong. Guy Gray replied for the losers. Craig Young's second goal of the game, in the second overtime period, propelled the Jets to a thrilling 7-6 win over the Breakers in the deciding game. Guy Gray also scored twice and singles came from Rob Varrin, Derek Dalley and Mel Best. Andy Sullivan and Ward Gosse each scored two for Southern Shore, who also had singles from Bill Windsor and Brendan Coady.

1995

The central league ceased operation for the 1994-95 season, forcing the Gander Flyers to compete in the Avalon West league, thus leaving the two Avalon winners to battle for the Herder Trophy. Andy Sullivan repeated as scoring champion for a record-setting fifth time with 100 points, just ahead of teammate Bill Windsor with 84. Bill Windsor was named winner of the Gus Soper award as the circuit's most valuable player. Peter White of Flatrock was the top goaltender with a 1.58 average and two shutouts, while teammate Robert Bradbury was second in Avalon East scoring and captured the Howie Clouter award for the year. Outer Cove's Trevor Boland was named rookie of the year and the Evening Telegram Trophy was once again won by the Southern Shore Breakers. Flatrock defeated Outer Cove in four straight games and Torbay eliminated Portugal Cove by the same result as both teams advanced to the Avalon East final and Herder semi-final. In the Avalon West league, Southern Shore stopped Bell Island in four games, while the St. John's Capitals needed all seven games to edge the Gander Flyers four games to three.

Scott Sullivan and Andy Sullivan each scored three goals with Bill Windsor adding a pair as Southern Shore stopped St. John's 11-4 to open their series. Andy Sullivan had another three-goal game and added three assists as the Breakers won the second game 9-3. Jason Courtney, Steve Scott and Gary Sullivan each scored twice with Southern Shore winning game three 8-2. The Breakers, with three goals from Scott Sullivan and two from Jason Courtney, clinched a berth in the final with a 9-4 decision in the fourth game. Flatrock were just as dominant in the eastern playoffs as they defeated Torbay four games to one. Upon opening with a 4-2 decision, Robert Bradbury had a pair of two-goal games as Flatrock won 4-3 and 3-2 to take a 3-0 lead in the series. With Torbay doubling the Flyers 6-3 for their only victory, Flatrock advanced to the Herder final with a 4-1 victory.

Two-goal performances by Bill Windsor, Andy and Gary Sullivan led the Breakers to a 9-6 victory in the opening game of the final. Steve Scott, Scott Sullivan and Chris O'Keefe chipped in with singles as Robert Bradbury was tops for the Flyers with a pair of goals. Singles came from Kirby Dumaresque, Lee Hawco, Ed Oates and Warren Sullivan. Series MVP Jamie Coady pulled the trigger on four goals to lead the

Breakers to a 6-4 victory in the second game. Steve Scott and Jason Courtney also scored, while Flatrock had goals from Kirby Dumaresque, Hubert Hutton, Craig Squires and Tony Hawco. Jamie Coady rifled two more goals in game three as Southern Shore won 5-3. Scott Sullivan, Chris Davis and Bill Windsor added singles. Kirby Dumaresque scored with two and Craig Squires netted one for the Flyers. Southern Shore completed a sweep of the final by dumping Flatrock 7-2 in the fourth game. Andy Sullivan led the way with two goals, while Steve Scott and Gary Sullivan, Jamie Coady, Loyola O'Driscoll and Jason Courtney rounded out the scoring. Craig Squires and Joey Maynard had the only goals for Flatrock.

1996

The 1996 provincial playoffs offered a repeat of the previous year with the Southern Shore Breakers and the Flatrock Flyers squared off once again to determine the Herder Memorial Trophy champions. In Avalon East, Flatrock disposed of Portugal Cove in four straight games, while Torbay got by Pouch Cove four games to two. In the west, the St. John's Capitals (winners of the Evening Telegram Trophy) overcame the stellar goaltending of Craig Courtney to stop Bell Island four games to two, while the Breakers came from a 3-1 deficit to upset the Conception Bay CeeBees four games to three. Denis Strong of the CeeBees was the league's top scorer with 27 goals and 32 assists for 59 points and Flatrock's Blair Langmead was the top goal-tender with a 1.75 average. Devon Penney of Bell Island picked up two awards when he was named the rookie of the year and

Blair Langmead

the most gentlemanly and effective player. Kevin Fitzpatrick of Torbay walked off with most valuable player honours.

Andy Sullivan had a goal and two assists to lead Southern Shore past St. John's 5-4 in the Avalon West final. Scott Sullivan pulled the trigger on two goals as the Breakers won the second game 5-3, with Bill Morrissey scoring two goals in a losing cause. Two-goal efforts from Bill Morrissey, Mike Tilley and Russ Kennedy earned the Capitals a 7-4 decision in the third game,

133

but Andy Sullivan counted twice and Loyola O'Driscoll potted the winner as the Breakers edged the Capitals 3-1 in game four. Andy Sullivan, Bill Windsor and Barry Sullivan each had a goal and two assists as Southern Shore advanced to the final with a 5-3 victory over the Capitals.

Kirby Dumaresque fired two goals as Flatrock edged Torbay 3-2 to open the eastern final, but Kevin Fitzpatrick's second-overtime goal (his second of the game), lifted Torbay to a 5-4 win in game two. Kirby Dumaresque scored a goal and assisted on two more as Flatrock took the lead with a 3-1 triumph. Flatrock moved closer to the final with a 6-0 victory in game four as Peter White blocked 20 shots for the shutout and Robert Bradbury netted two goals. Jack Kane's hat-trick sparked Flatrock to a 5-1 victory that clinched a berth in the Herder final.

Robert Bradbury continued his torrid scoring with two goals as Flatrock opened the final with a 4-2 victory over the Breakers. Single goals came from Kirby Dumaresque and Craig Squires, with Ward Gosse and Don Roche scoring for the losers. Robert Bradbury connected on two more goals, while Kirby Dumaresque and Ed Tapper chipped in with singles to give Flatrock a 4-3 victory in game two. Andy Sullivan scored twice for the Breakers and assisted on Loyola O'Driscoll's marker. Chris Davis and Terry Peddle each scored twice and Bill Windsor had one as Southern Shore stopped Flatrock 5-2 in game three. Ed Oates had both Flatrock goals. Scott Sullivan scored twice and singles came from Andy Sullivan, Terry Peddle, Chris O'Keefe, Roger Ryan and Don Roche as Southern Shore tied the series with a 7-2 win. Ed Oates and Ed Tapper replied for the Flyers. Flatrock found themselves down three games to two after losing game five 4-2. For the Breakers, Bill Windsor led the attack with two goals, Brent Sullivan added a single and Andy Sullivan counted for a single and three assists. Joey Maynard and Kirby Dumaresque scored for Flatrock. The Flyers forced the series to a seventh game by upsetting Southern Shore 7-5 in the sixth game in Mobile. Robert Bradbury connected on two goals for the winners who got one apiece from Lee and Tony Hawco, Ed Oates, Kirby Dumaresque and Ed Tapper. Andy Sullivan, Bill Windsor, Terry Peddle, Chris Davis and Roger Ryan did the scoring for the Breakers. A five-goal outburst in the first period proved to be the difference as Southern Shore won its second straight Herder with a 9-2 victory over Flatrock before a packed house at Feildian Gardens. Terry Peddle paced the winners with three goals and Chris Davis chipped in with a pair. Singles came from David Walsh, Bill Windsor, Scott Sullivan and Loyola O'Driscoll. Hubert Hutton and Steve Cleary scored in the first period for the losers.

1997

With the revival of the central senior league, three leagues were set to play for the Herder Memorial Trophy in 1997. Badger stopped Lewisporte in the final to emerge as champions in the central division, while Flatrock repeated as champions of Avalon East by defeating Outer Cove and Torbay. In the Avalon West league, St. John's upset defending champion Southern Shore four games to two and toppled the Conception Bay CeeBees in six games. Derek Dalley of the Twillingate Combines was the league scoring champion with 19 goals and 26 assists for 45 points in 11 games, while Kirby Dumaresque of Flatrock was named the most valuable player. Teammate Peter White took the top goaltending award with a 2.00 average, while Bill Windsor of Southern Shore was the Howie Clouter award winner and teammate Jamie Tobin was named the top rookie. Flatrock captured the Evening Telegram trophy with the best overall percentage during regular season play.

Bill Windsor

Two-goal performances by John Drover, Denis Strong and David Button lifted the CeeBees to a 10-7 win over St. John's in the first game of their series. Bob Pardy had three goals in a losing cause. Rick Field and Trevor Boland each had four goals and Corey Power had two goals and three assists as the Capitals evened the series with a 17-3 victory. Rick Field notched another pair in game three as the Capitals won 7-3. Marty Woodford, Todd Hutchings and Mike O'Neil had two goals apiece to give the Capitals a 9-2 victory in game four. Neil Cleary's three goals kept the CeeBees alive with a 6-4 decision in the fifth game, but the Caps clinched a berth in the Herder semi-final with a 12-3 win in game six as Trevor Boland, Rick Field and Don Jarvis scored two goals each.

Flatrock disposed of Torbay in four straight games to capture the Avalon East title. Kirby Dumaresque had a goal and an assist as the Flyers won the opening game of the best-of-seven series 4-2 and Steve Cleary fired two goals in a 4-2 win in game two. Robert Bradbury netted three points in a 5-1 decision in game three and Ed Oates had a pair of goals in a 9-2 romp to sweep the series.

Flatrock came from behind with four goals in the third period and got a goal from Ed Oates in the second overtime to edge St. John's 9-8 to open the best-of-seven Herder semi-final.

Ed Oates

Ed Tapper and Robert Bradbury each collected two goals, while singles came from Steve Cleary, Al Wozney, Joey Maynard and Graham Squires. Rob O'Brien, Chad Benson and Corey Power had two goals apiece for the Capitals, with singles coming from P.J. Power and Todd Hutchings. The Flyers took the second game by a 5-2 score on goals by Ed Oates, Robert Bradbury, Joey Maynard, Steve Cleary and Al Wozney, while Todd Hutchings and Corey Power replied for the losers. Flatrock took a stranglehold on the series with a 5-4 win in overtime in game three. Lee Hawco, who also had two assists, netted the eventual winner, while Steve Cleary had two markers and Jack Kane and Kirby Dumaresque netted singles. Bob Pardy, Don Powell, Brad Stephens and Rick Field scored for the Capitals. St. John's staved off elimination to win game four 11-3 with Don Powell netting three goals and Corey Power and Todd Hutchings adding two each. Goals by Ed Tapper, Robert Bradbury and Joey Maynard lifted the Flyers to the series win with a 3-2 victory in the fifth game to advance to the Herder final. Trevor Boland and Chad Benson had the goals for the losers.

In the opening game of the best-of-five Herder final, Flatrock broke open a tie game with a pair of third-period goals to down Badger 5-3. John Bolger and Al Wozney led the winners with two goals apiece and Jack Kane had one. Craig Loder, Craig Tulk and Rob Penney were the Badger goalgetters. Two goals by Kirby Dumaresque and singles by Tony Hawco and Steve Cleary backed the 20-save shutout goaltending of Blair

136

Langmead as Flatrock won the second contest 4-0. They swept to their second Herder Trophy with a 5-1 victory in the third game on goals by Ed Oates, Joey Maynard, Lee Hawco, Kirby Dumaresque and Jack Kane. Dave Walbourne had the only goal for Badger.

1998

It was the same old story in Avalon East in 1998 as Flatrock again defeated Torbay to advance to the Herder semi-final. Southern Shore regained control of the Avalon West final by stopping the Conception Bay CeeBees in four straight games, while Badger repeated in the central league by defeating Bishop's Falls. Scott Sullivan of Southern Shore tallied 117 points to edge teammate Corey Power by one point for the scoring title. Scott Sullivan was also named the league's most valuable player. Blair Langmead of Flatrock was the top goalie with an 0.92 average after allowing only 11 goals in 12 games and posting five shutouts. Southern Shore led the Avalon West league during the season to claim the Telegram trophy and Flatrock team captain Robert Bradbury was named winner of the Howie Clouter award for the second time. The rookie of the year award went to Mark Robinson of the Conception Bay North Tigers who finished the season with 47 goals and 45 assists for 92 points.

Badger, Flatrock and Southern Shore competed in semi-final play in a home-and-home series, with the top two finishers earning a berth in the Herder final. Badger opened the series with a 2-1 victory over Flatrock on goals by Shawn Glavine and Dennis Power. Kirby Dumaresque replied for the Flyers. Andre Cornick's overtime goal gave the Bombers a 6-5 triumph over Southern Shore in the second game. He also scored in regulation time as did Juan Strickland, Shawn Glavine, Scott Bishop and Jamie White. Corey Power and Steve Scott each had two for the Breakers and Darrell Walsh added a single. Derek Sullivan had two goals and Scott Sullivan netted one and three assists as Southern Shore blanked Flatrock 7-0 behind the goaltending of Chris Browne. Corey Power, Don Crane, Bill Windsor and Junior Farrell also scored for the Breakers. Flatrock staved off elimination with a 7-4 win over Southern Shore in their return match. Kirby Dumaresque and Steve Cleary notched two goals apiece, while Ed Oates, Joey Maynard and Robert Bradbury added singles. Corey Power had two, while Don Crane and Scott Sullivan scored the others for the losers. Corey Power netted two goals and Dennis Lake blocked 16 shots as Southern Shore gained a berth in the final by stopping Badger 3-0. Brent Sullivan tallied the other goal.

The second berth was decided in the final game and Flatrock had to defeat Badger by two goals to advance. Ed Oates took matters into his own hands with three goals as the Flyers won 5-1. Warren Sullivan and Robert Bradbury also scored for Flatrock in the rough and tumble game that saw both benches clear in the final period. Shawn Glavine had the lone goal for Badger.

The seven-game final between Southern Shore and Flatrock was one of the most entertaining in the long and tremendous history of the Herder Memorial Trophy. Capacity crowds filled the Southern Shore Arena in Mobile and Feildian Gardens in St. John's to view the series. Ed Oates and Kirby Dumaresque each fired two goals as Flatrock opened the series with a 7-3 victory. Todd McDonald, Robert Bradbury and Jamie Tobin also scored. Steve Scott, David Walsh and Don Crane replied for Southern Shore. Goals by Junior Farrell, Steve Scott, Bill Windsor, and Brent and Scott Sullivan lifted the Breakers to a 5-3 decision in game two. Todd McDonald, Kirby Dumaresque and Robert Bradbury scored for the losers. Scott Sullivan netted three goals and Bill Windsor added two as Southern Shore took the series lead with an 8-6 victory. Paul Brazil, Corey Power and Don Crane chipped in with singles. Ed Oates and Steve Cleary each scored twice for Flatrock, with singles coming from Kirby Dumaresque and Chris Sweet. The Flyers battled back to tie the series with a 6-4 win in game four. Robert Bradbury and Ed Oates each had two goals and two assists, while Kirby Dumaresque had a goal and three setups and Jamie Tobin notched the other tally. Steve Scott had two for the Breakers and Junior Farrell and Don Crane added one apiece. Southern Shore goaltender Denis Lake was called upon to make only 19 saves. Brent Sullivan paced the Breakers' win with two goals as the team moved to within one win of the Herder with a 4-0 victory in game five. Bill Windsor and Scott Sullivan also scored. Flatrock stayed alive in the series with a 5-3 victory in game six as Al Wozney scored two goals. Singles came from Lee Hawco, Ed Oates and Mike James. Scott Sullivan, Barry Sullivan and Don Crane replied for the Breakers.

Game seven was a classic and exciting encounter before more than 1,500 fans in Mobile that didn't see a minor penalty called. The partisan Southern Shore crowd was silenced in the opening period as Joey Maynard, with two, and Kirby Dumaresque, with one, scored for Flatrock to take a 3-0 lead. However, the Breakers battled back on goals by Junior Farrell, John O'Driscoll and Brent Sullivan to have the game tied 3-3 heading into the third period. The teams battled through a scoreless frame until an overtime goal by Kirby Dumaresque (from a scramble in front of Denis Lake) sent the Flatrock fans wild and gave the Flyers their second straight Herder.

Kirby Dumaresque

1999

Southern Shore, Badger and Flatrock all repeated as champions of their respective leagues and met again in 1999 for the Herder playoffs. Southern Shore had an easy time knocking off the Goulds Pacers and the Conception Bay North Tigers to claim the Avalon West title, while Flatrock lost only one game in eliminating the Conception Bay Central Ironworkers and Torbay for yet another time. Badger got by Stephenville to claim the other spot. Ed Russell of the Conception Bay Tigers was the league's top scorer with 71 points and he also picked up the rookie of the year award. The Howie Clouter award went to Brent Sullivan of the Southern Shore Breakers, while Blair Langmead of Flatrock posted a 1.92 goals against average to repeat as the top goaltender. Steve Mifflin of the Conception Bay Central Ironworkers was named the circuit's most valuable player. Badger claimed the Telegram Trophy for a first-place finish in the central-west league.

Southern Shore, having failed to win the Herder for the two previous years, lured scoring star Andy Sullivan out of retirement for the playoffs. Sullivan was instrumental in the playoff run, leading the Breakers to 15 straight victories in post-season play without a loss. In addition to sweeping the Pacers and the Tigers, Southern Shore won all four games in the round robin semi-final and dropped the Badger Bombers, the central champions, in three games in the best-of-five final to regain the

Herder Memorial trophy. Flatrock eliminated the Conception Bay Central Ironworkers and Torbay to reach the Herder semi-final.

Shawn Glavine and Corey Hemeon each netted a pair of goals as Badger opened the semi-final with a 7-2 win over Flatrock. Bill Armstrong, Andre Cornick and Wade Sutton also scored for the winners. Steve Cleary and Al Wozney scored for the Flyers. Shannon Colbert scored two third-period goals to lift Southern Shore to a 5-3 win over Flatrock. Chris O'Keefe also had two for the winners and Brent Sullivan added the other. Kirby Dumaresque had two goals and Ed Oates a goal and two assists for the Flyers. Southern Shore doubled Badger 4-2 to win its second game as Scott Sullivan notched a pair of markers. Steve Scott and Loyola O'Driscoll each had one. Wade Sutton and Paul Pittman scored for Badger. Southern Shore clinched a berth in the final by dumping Flatrock 7-3 with Steve Scott and Shannon Colbert each scoring twice and Andy Sullivan adding a goal and three assists. Brent Sullivan and Chris O'Keefe added singles. Joey Maynard, Paul Crane and Joe Boland had the only goals for the losers. Brent Sullivan had two goals and Scott Sullivan chipped in with a goal and three helpers in a 7-1 victory for Southern Shore over Badger. Don Gosse, Bill Windsor, Derek Sullivan and Steve Scott also scored. Shawn Glavine replied for the Bombers. Paul Pittman had two goals as Badger came from behind to stop Flatrock 4-2 to clinch the second spot in the final. Scott Young and Scott Stuckless also scored, while Ed Oates and Kirby Dumaresque scored for Flatrock.

Andy Sullivan

Steve Scott fired two goals and assisted on two more to lead Southern Shore to an 8-1 victory over Badger in the opening game of the final. Barry, Scott and Andy Sullivan, Darryl Costello, Bill Windsor and Loyola O'Driscoll added singles. Scott Bishop netted the lone Badger goal. Bishop went on to score the only Badger goal in game two, a 6-1 setback to the Breakers who received single tallies from Junior Farrell, Bill Windsor, Cory Bond, Brent, Barry and Andy Sullivan. The Breakers clinched their first Herder in front of their hometown fans with a 6-3 victory in the third game. Brent Sullivan pulled the trigger on three goals, while Scott Sullivan had two goals and two assists. Andy Sullivan completed the scoring. Wade Sutton, Shawn Glavine and Corey Power replied for the Bombers.

The St. John's teams have dominated the battle for the Herder, winning 19 of the 62 championships. St. Bon's won the title ten times, the St. John's Capitals seven, the Blue Caps and Mike's Shamrocks one apiece. The Grand Falls All-stars, Andcos and Cataracts have posted ten victories, while the Corner Brook Royals have nine Herders to their credit. The Buchans Miners are next with five wins and the Conception Bay CeeBees have four. The Flatrock Flyers and the Southern Shore Breakers have each recorded three wins on the coveted trophy, while the Bell Island Miners, the Gander Flyers and the Stephenville Jets have each won twice. The Port aux Basques Mariners, the Badger Bombers and the La Scie Jets have one victory apiece. The Bay Roberts Rovers, the Labrador City Carol Lakers, the Clarenville Caribous, the Bonavista Cabots, the Mount Pearl Blades and the Memorial University Beothucks have also participated in the Herder playoffs, but weren't successful in having their names inscribed on the prestigious Herder Memorial Trophy.

SCREECH

a Newfoundland tradition

salutes

the

publishers

of

OUR SPORTS HERITAGE

MAVERICK
SPORT COLLECTABLES

Sportscards & Supplies • Memorabilia
Autographs • Souvenirs • Coins
and lots more

An official supplier of all
St. John's Maple Leafs
souvenirs and clothing.

We do mail order!

243 Duckworth Street
St. John's, NF
A1C 1G8
(709) 738-2888
acorbett@thezone.net

Moores, Andrews

BARRISTERS, SOLICITORS, NOTARIES PUBLIC

A. Douglas Moores, Q.C.
David L. G. Andrews, B.Sc. (Hon.), L.L.B., G.D.Ed. (P.)
Richard L. Collins, B.A. (Hon.), LL.B

We Handle All Injury Claims

Preferred Areas of Practice
Personal Injury • Criminal Law • Real Estate
Estates and Probates • Commercial

Conception Bay's Oldest
Established Law Firm

P.O. Box 806
Conception Bay Highway
Bay Roberts, NF A0A 1G0
Tel: (709) 786-7114 • Fax: (709) 786-6952

A *The Herder Champions*

1935 - Corner Brook Royals
Ron Taaffe (general manager), Gerry Edens (manager), Will Fitzpatrick, Tony Ledrew, Hal Cross, Fred Power, Frank Byrne, Jack Downey, Hal Power

1936 - St. Bon's
Frank "Dee" Donnelly (coach), Art Hamlyn, Gerry Hanley, Gordon Halley, Dick Furlong, Frank "Andy" Cahill, Basil Hutton, Bern Maher, Bob Godden, Charlie Godden, Ed Brophy, Jack Maher, Jim Norris

1937 - St. Bon's
Frank "Dee" Donnelly (coach), Art Hamlyn, Dick Furlong, Gerry Hanley, Charlie Godden, Frank "Andy" Cahill, Jim Vinnicombe, Basil Hutton, Len Walsh, Jim Edstrom, Jack Maher, Ed Brophy, Bernard Collins, Ed Furlong, Peter Henley, Ed Berrigan

1938 - St. Bon's
Frank "Dee" Donnelly (coach), Syd Thompson, Dick Furlong, Gerry Hanley, Jack Vinnicombe, Frank "Andy" Cahill, Basil Hutton, Ed Berrigan, Al Felix, Kev Brophy, Jim Edstrom, Ferd Graham, Peter Henley, Bob Simms, Bernard Collins, Dick Byrne

1939 - St. Bon's
Frank "Dee" Donnelly (coach), Dick Furlong, Syd Thompson, Bernard Collins, Wick Collins, Frank "Andy" Cahill, Jack Vinnicombe, Cec Penney, Les O'Reilly, Brian Walsh, Bill Harris, John Veitch, Jim Foley, Fred Thompson, Dick Byrne, Frank Gamberg, Kev Brophy, Jack Dunne

1940 - St. Bon's
Frank "Dee" Donnelly (coach), Syd Thompson, Dick Furlong, Jack Dunne, Wick Collins, Jack Vinnicombe, Frank "Andy" Cahill, Les O'Reilly, Bill Harris, Brian Walsh, Cec Penney, Bernard Collins, John Veitch, Jim Foley, John Finn, Derm O'Driscoll, Frank Gamberg

1941 - Bell Island

Reid Proudfoot (coach), Gordon Edwards, Frank Gamberg, Bill Lindsay, Lorne Proudfoot, Gordon Normore, Hugh Connors, Ned Penney, Bob Petrie, Gordon Petrie, Gus Normore

1942 - No competition

1943 - No competition

1944 - Bell Island

Reid Proudfoot (coach), Gordon Neary, Gordon Highmore, Gordon Rees, Gus Normore, Gordon Normore, Gordon Edwards, Leo Power, Ned Penney, Bob Petrie, Brian Murphy, Hugh Connors

1945 - St. Bon's

Bill Harris (playing-coach), Frank Gamberg, Myles Furlong, Jack Dunne, Bob Furlong, Peter O'Mara, Bill Power, Cyril Power, Noel Vinnicombe, Jack Walsh, Hugh Fardy, Cec Penney, Bill Corbett, John Doyle, Terry Trainor, Jack Vinnicombe

1946 - St. Bon's

Bill Harris (playing-coach), Bill Corbett, Ted Gillies, Terry Trainor, Fa Murphy, Jim Kielly, Cyril Power, Myles Furlong, Hugh Fardy, Frank Gamberg, Noel Vinnicombe, Bill Power, John Doyle, Jack Reardigan

1947 - St. Bon's

Frank "Dee" Donnelly (coach), Frank Gamberg, John Doyle, Myles Furlong, Terry Trainor, Hugh Fardy, Bill Power, Noel Vinnicombe, Cyril Power, Fa Murphy, Ted Withers, Bill Harris, Jack Reardigan, Ed Murphy

1948 - St. Bon's

Frank "Dee" Donnelly (coach), Hugh Fardy, Myles Furlong, Fa Murphy, Noel Vinnicombe, Jack Reardigan, Bill Furlong, Frank Gamberg, Jack Ryan, Ted Withers, Terry Trainor, Bill Corbett, John Doyle, Cyril Power, Bill Harris, Ted Gillies, Hugh Conway, Ed Murphy

1949 - St. Bon's

Frank "Dee" Donnelly (coach), John Doyle, Frank Gamberg, Myles Furlong, Hugh Fardy, Ted Gillies, Fa Murphy, Jim McNamara, Cyril Power, Noel Vinnicombe, Ted Withers, Jack Reardigan, Bill Corbett, Jack Ryan, Hugh Conway

1950 - Buchans Miners

Frank Bowman (playing-coach), Bill Scott, Roy Mullins, Red Croteau, Ken Joy, Art "Copper" Laite, Jim Hornell, Paul "Scottie" McPhail, Al Mullins, Tom Barrett, Herb Pike, George Pike, Bob Piercey

1951 - Buchans Miners

Frank Bowman (playing-coach), Allie Carver, Bernie "Bessie" MacDonald, Jim Hornell, Willie Robertson, George Pike, Herb Pike, Bill Scott, Paul "Scottie" McPhail, Al Mullins, Ron Mullins, Bob Piercey, Ray Marshall, Bill Kelly, Ken Joy

1952 - Buchans Miners

Frank Bowman (playing-coach), Bill Scott, Willie Robertson, Allie Carver, Al Mullins, Bob McKinley, Bill Kelly, Herb Pike, Ray Morrison, Jim Hornell, George Pike, Ron Mullins, Brian Mitchell, Bob Piercey, Jim "Sham" McInnis

1953 - Grand Falls all-stars

Wes Trainor (playing-coach), Gerald "Markie" Andrews, Roy Byrne, Doug Foote, Dave Green, Fred Sanger, Clar Goulding, George Howse, Ray Marshall, Joe Byrne, George Faulkner, Al Folkes, Jim "Buck" Hannaford, Wats Goobie, Dave Jackson

1954 - Buchans Miners

Frank Bowman (playing-coach), Gerry Casey, Hugh Wadden, Jim Hornell, Danny McNeil, Bill Scott, Herb Pike, Bill Harris, Al Mullins, Ron Mullins, Jim "Sham" McInnis, Pat Kennedy, Tony Walsh, Jack Cooper, Tom Loder, Tubby St. George, Lloyd Soper, Roy Mullins

1955 - Grand Falls Andcos

Wes Trainor (playing-coach), George Howse, Fred Sanger, Clar Goulding, Wats Goobie, Al Folkes, Clobie Collins, Jim "Sham" McInnis, Neil Amadio, Cec Thomas, Jim "Buck" Hannaford, Jack MacKenzie, Gerald "Markie" Andrews, Alex Faulkner, Vic Grignon

1956 - Grand Falls Andcos

Wes Trainor (playing-coach), Jim "Sham" McInnis, Rollie Clarke, Fred Foley, George Howse, Harvey Howse, Gerald "Markie" Andrews, Alex Faulkner, Jack MacKenzie, Clobie Collins, Jim "Buck" Hannaford, Vic Grignon, Al Folkes, Wats Goobie, Clar Goulding, Roy Byrne

1957 - Grand Falls Andcos

Wes Trainor (playing-coach), Jim "Sham" McInnis, Jim "Corp" Janes, Mun Pond, Terry Jesseau, Cec Thomas, Fred Foley, Harvey Howse, George Howse, Clar Goulding, Clobie Collins, Alex Faulkner, Lindy Faulkner, Wats Goobie, Jim "Buck" Hannaford, Vic Grignon, Neil Knight, Jim Temple, Heber Rideout, Gerald "Markie" Andrews

1958 - Grand Falls Andcos

Wes Trainor (playing-coach), Dick Duder, Orin Carver, Don Penton, Sherm White, Tom Blackmore, Eric Cumby, Warren Eastman, Ollie Tulk, Roy Davis, Jim Barker, Bill McGettigan, Cec Thomas, Jim Kennedy, Roger Dean, Cyril Power, Pat Corbin, Alfie Hiscock, Ralph Cook

1959 - Grand Falls Andcos

Ray LaCroix (playing-coach), Sam Gregory, Tom Blackmore, Alfie Hiscock, Gerald "Markie" Andrews, Bob Snow, Jim "Buck" Hannaford, Al Edwards, Terry Jesseau, Harvey Howse, Cec Thomas, Jim Dawe, Sid Paddick, Bob Davis, Jim McDonald, Jim "Sham" McInnis, Eddie Power

1960 - Conception Bay CeeBees

George Faulkner (playing-coach), Alex Faulkner, Allan Dawe, Bill MacDonald, Carl Penney, Jim Penney, Jim Kennedy, John Thomey, Alfie Hiscock, Jim Coady, Frank Fleming, Jack Faulkner, Fred Rossiter, Bill Sullivan, Ed Pumphrey

1961 - Conception Bay CeeBees

George Faulkner (playing-coach), Doug Foote, Jim Kennedy, Fred Pardy, Frank Fleming, Mike Kelly, Alfie Hiscock, Bern Fitzpatrick, Carl Penney, Jim Penney, Jack Faulkner, Brian Wakelin, Jim Coady, Ed Dawe, Don Pierce

1962 - Corner Brook Royals

Frank Dorrington (playing-coach), Fred Randell, Bob Marshall, Dick Power, Clobie Collins, Ed O'Quinn, Francis Walsh, Fa Murphy, Willis French, Bob Smith, George Boljkovac, John Madinsky, Doug Hillman, Orin Carver, Mike Brothers, Ed Lawrence, Jim Grant

1963 - Buchans Miners

Neil Amadio (playing-coach), Terry Booth, Ern Laite, Bill Scott, Jerry Brockie, Gordie Butler, Mike Kelly, Hugh Wadden, Frank

Walker, Mort Verbiski, Ed Kelly, Frank Finlayson, Fred Pardy, Tubby St. George, Bill Lush, Martin Craig, Bill Harris, Tony Head

1964 - Corner Brook Royals
Frank Dorrington (playing-coach), Mike Brothers, Clobie Collins, Fred Randell, Bert Brake, Dave Pardy, Ed Lawrence, Ray Murphy, Francis Walsh, Hec Caines, Jake Critch, John Carter, Harry Katrynuk, Ed O'Quinn, George Aucoin, Mickey Walsh

1965 - Conception Bay CeeBees
George Faulkner (playing-coach), Harry Hunt, Alex Faulkner, Jim Dawe, Mac Martin, Terry Matthews, Jim Penney, Carl Penney, Ern Cole, John Fitzgerald, Gerry Lahey, Jack Faulkner, Harold Stanley, Hubert Hutton

1966 - Corner Brook Royals
Frank Dorrington (playing-coach), Don Clarke, Mickey Walsh, Jim Guy, Bert Brake, Harry Katrynuk, Jim Kennedy, Clobie Collins, Ed O'Quinn, Rob Mainwaring, Ed Lawrence, Francis Walsh, Ernie Hynes, Fred Randell, Bob Smith, Rollie Clarke, Tony Keough, Jake Critch

1967 - Conception Bay CeeBees
George Faulkner (playing-coach), Carl Penney, Gary Simmons, Jim Penney, Mac Martin, Bern Fitzpatrick, Doug Moores, Nev Pike, Jim Hartling, Gerry Lahey, Don Crane, John Fitzgerald, Joe Hunt, Jim Dawe, Doug Sheppard, Peter Babb

1968 - Corner Brook Royals
Frank Dorrington (playing-coach), Jim Guy, Jake Critch, Alex King, Reg Asselin, Ernie Hynes, Francis Walsh, Ed Lawrence, Tim Rothwell, Bob Clarke, Foster Lamswood, Doug Grant, Joe Lundrigan, Jim Kennedy, Doug Sheppard, Ed O'Quinn

1969 - Gander Flyers
Jacques Allard (playing-coach), Brian Rafuse, Stan Cook, Pat Shallow, Mike Anderson, Harry Katrynuk, Tom Smythe, Pat Penney, Bill Lastic, J. C. Garneau, Leo Kane, Jack Faulkner, Mike Kelly, Dennis Mullins, Ed Philpott

1970 - St. John's Capitals
Howie Meeker (coach), Les Calder (playing-coach), Bob Warr, Doug Squires, Jim Penney, George Spracklin, Stan Cook, Bill Malone, Eg Billard, Mike Donovan, Bern Fitzpatrick, Don Quinn, John McCallum, Bruce Butler, Bob Badcock, Ray Murphy, Phil

McDonald, Jack Hill, Dave Kendall, Derm Connolly, Hubert Hutton, Ford Metcalfe, Gar Pynn, Mike Fitzpatrick

1971 - Grand Falls Cataracts

Marc Pichette (coach), Leo Murphy, Jean Guy Morrissette, Jim Beckman, Harry Katrynuk, Al Dwyer, Roger Bowers, Jim Dawe, Roger Dwyer, Alf Ellis, Jim Temple, Frank Finlayson, Al Bargery, Harold Stanley, Lloyd "Toy Toy" Gallant, Roger Martin, Fred Janes, Denis Murphy, Walt Davis

1972 - Grand Falls Cataracts

Marc Pichette (coach), Al Dwyer, Jim Beckman, Frank Finlayson, Alf Ellis, Jean Guy Morrissette, Jim Munch, Terry French, Tony White, Jim Dawe, Harold Stanley, Tony Grimes, Terry Sheppard, Al Bargery, Don Howse, Fred Janes, Leo Murphy, Jim Temple, Harry Katrynuk, Roger Bowers

1973 - St. John's Capitals

Bob Badcock (coach), Doug Atkinson, Pat Dempsey, John Lester, Bob Lambert, Nigel Facey, Rick Babstock, Hubert Hutton, Randy Pearcey, Sandy Gibbons, Derek Hancock, Charlie Greene, Ford Metcalfe, Bern Fitzpatrick, Derm Connolly, Gary Connolly, Bob Hutton, Bill Driscoll, Jerry Power

1974 - St. John's Capitals

Bob Badcock (coach), Tols Chapman, Pat Dempsey, John Lester, Don Quinn, Greg Pearcey, Hubert Hutton, Nigel Facey, Bob Lambert, Rick Babstock, Charlie Babstock, Dan Noftall, Brian Mulcahy, Max Hayes, John McCallum, Ford Metcalfe, Brian Brocklehurst, Jack Hill, Sandy Gibbons, Jerry Power, Bob Hutton, Randy Pearcey, Derm Connolly, Gary Connolly, Derek Hancock

1975 - St. John's Capitals

Bob Badcock (coach), Randy Pearcey, Brian Mulcahy, George Faulkner, Bob Faulkner, Erik Seaward, Sandy Gibbons, Greg Pearcey, Max Hayes, Jim Heale, Ed James, Nigel Facey, Dan Noftall, Glen Critch, Tols Chapman, Pat Dempsey, Derek Hancock, John Lester, Bob Lambert, Don Quinn, Hubert Hutton, Rick Babstock, Charlie Babstock, Jerry Power, Ed Kent, John McCallum, Dave Power

1976 - St. John's Capitals

George Faulkner (coach), Pat Dempsey, Doug Atkinson, Brian Gibbons, Jim Wilcox, Hubert Hutton, Greg Pearcey, Don Quinn, Dan Noftall, Rick Babstock, Randy Pearcey, Nigel Facey, Charlie

Greene, Charlie Babstock, Glen Critch, Ed James, Max Hayes, Jim Heale, Brian Mulcahy, Dave Power, Jerry Power

1977 - Corner Brook Royals

Frank "Danky" Dorrington (coach), Ernie Hynes, Alex Blanchard, Terry Gillam, Ted McComb, Rick Boone, Joe Lundrigan, Jim Guy, Bill Perry, Paul Althouse, Jim Roche, Alex King, Dave Kennedy, Alvin Park, Brent Griffin, Mark Roberts, Bram Pike

1978 - St. John's Blue Caps

Bill Clarke (coach), Jim Heale, Pat Dempsey, Dave Buckingham, Charlie Babstock, Derek Hancock, Mike O'Handley, Randy Pearcey, Sandy Gibbons, Jim Mullett, Charlie Greene, Rick Babstock, Tony Pearcey, Don Quinn, Ed Philpott, Tom Kinsella, Erik Seaward, Gerry Fagan, Greg Pearcey

1979 - St. John's Mike's Shamrocks

Jim Byrne (coach), George Faulkner (coach), Junior Hammond, Fred Burke, Nigel Facey, Bob O'Neill, Hubert Hutton, John Breen, Bill Breen, Bill Perry, Ron Cadigan, Brian Mulcahy, Gary Noftle, John Hearn, Mark Idler, Max Hayes, Grant MacDougall, John Byrne, Paul Norman, Gary Connolly, Derm Connolly, Jerry Power, Bob Faulkner

1980 - Gander Flyers

Jack Faulkner (coach), Zane Forbes, Dave Ivany, Kirk Johnson, Reg Batson, Keith Elliott, Tom Rafuse, Gerry McCarron, Ed Philpott, Kevin Kelly, Doug Batson, Ted Mercer, Dennis Laing, Jim Mullett, Dave Mercer, Mike McNiven, Terry John, Bruce Sparkes, John McKay, Paul Richardson

1981 - Grand Falls Cataracts

Joe Byrne (coach), Peter Sullivan, Reg Gulliford, Gord Gallant, Dan Flynn, Gene Faulkner, Ron Sweeney, Wayne Faulkner, George Penney, Laurie Cuvalier, Shawn Jewer, Tony Walsh, Tom Coolen, Tony Kennedy, Roger Elliott, Terry Head, Keith Boone, Larry O'Donnell, Mark Locken, Greg Byrne, Ed Davis

1982 - Grand Falls Cataracts

Joe Byrne (coach), Bruce Campbell, Ed Davis, Jacques Cormier, Harris Powell, Greg Byrne, Laurie Cuvalier, Gary Feener, Ron Sweeney, Tony Cuomo, Gord Gallant, Tony Walsh, Gene Faulkner, Steve Croucher, Wayne Faulkner, Tony Grimes, Bill Loughery, Keith Boone, Tom Coolen, Terry Cooke

1983 - Stephenville Jets

Larry Smith (coach), Don Howse (playing-coach), Juan Strickland, Bruce Campbell, Gary Dunville, Wayne Dove, Paul McInnis, Charlie Greene, Cal Dunville, Darren Pickrem, Terry Gillam, Craig Scott, Kevin Morrison, Steve Robson, Jim Cahoon, Roger Kennedy, Terry Billard, Wade Fitzpatrick, Kevin Miller, Wins Taylor, Kevin Pilgrim, Bill Perry, Tony White

1984 - Stephenville Jets

Larry Smith (coach), Don Howse (playing-coach), Sheldon Currie, Gary Dunville, Wayne Dove, Darren Pickrem, Zane Forbes, Kirk Johnson, Kevin Morrison, Jeff Leverman, Wayne Faulkner, Bob Young, Steve McKenzie, Ken Bruce, Bob Lambe, Kevin Miller, Jeff Smith, Mel Best, Don Rose, Steve Schumph, Bill Power, Bob Preston, Cal Dunville, Wade Fitzpatrick, Dave Slaney, Greg Byrne, Dave Priddle, Craig Anderson

1985 - Corner Brook Royals

Mike Anderson (coach), Kevin McCarthy, Whitney Richardson, Tony White, Tony Cuomo, Brad Fisher, Doug King, Ed Kearsey, Stan Hennigar, Terry Gillam, Steve Dunne, Kirk Johnson, Dan Cormier, Bob O'Neill, Ray Baird, Steve Gallant, Craig Kennedy, Dave Matte, Greg Hickey

1986 - Corner Brook Royals

Mike Anderson (coach), Terry Gillam (coach), Robbie Forbes, Gilbert Longpre, Ken Mercer, Todd Stark, Darryl Ulrich, Tim Cranston, Mark Jeffries, Dave Matte, Tony Cuomo, Dan Cormier, Stan Hennigar, Mac Tucker, Bill Breen, Bob O'Neill, Craig Kennedy, Byron Rideout, Kevin McCarthy, Kevin Lundrigan, Ray Baird, Don Bennett, Steve Gallant

1987 - St. John's Capitals

Bill Riley (playing-coach), Andy Sullivan, Hilton Ruggles, Peter White, Gerry Noftall, Russ Adam, Richard Linteau, Bill Walsh, Gus Greco, Ed Oates, Mac Tucker, Bob O'Neill, John Hutchings, Zane Forbes, Terry Wright, Kevin Bolger, Tony Walshe, Stan Hennigar, Graham Squires, Bob Thompson

1988 - Corner Brook Royals

Gus Greco (playing-coach), Craig Jenkins, Todd Stark, Dan Cormier, Ali Butorac, Marc Zeitlin, Jeff Regular, Robbie Forbes, Darren McWhirter, Chip Crandell, Dave Matte, Jeff Andrews, Ed Kearsey, Kevin McCarthy, Kev Lundrigan, Craig Payne, Shawn Green, Jamie Gallant

1989 - Port aux Basques Mariners

Ron Coleman (coach), Len Soccio, Juan Strickland, Marc West, Bill McDougall, Don Howse, Joe West, Dave McLay, Dwayne Joyce, John Witzke, Todd Savoury, Stewart Froude, Brian Burley, Chris Pusey, Greg Ware, Shawn Tobin, Rex Seaward, Terry McNeil, Barry Fudge, Glenn Allen, Richard Parsons

1990 - St. John's Capitals

Russ Adam (playing-coach), Andy Sullivan, Zane Forbes, Brad Fisher, Steve Joy, Peter Hanlon, Gerry Noftall, Dave Bennett, Ward Gosse, Bob Bugden, Kirby Dumaresque, Peter Jones, Don Howse, Roger Kennedy, Denis Lake, Kirk Fleming, Terry Hedderson, Chris Ryan, Paul Smith, Dean Mullett, Bob Thompson, Ian Norris, Jamie Gallant

1991 - No competition

1992 - Badger Bombers

Steve Croucher (coach), Hubie Hollett, Roger Kennedy, Dave Jacobs, George Penney, Barry Manuel, Bob Bugden, Gary Tulk, Steve Barnes, Greg Price, Craig Tulk, Perry Paul, Keith Evans, Keith Loder, Rod Howell, Barry Shugarue, Jerry Power, Harry Foley, Dave Butt, Greg Hayden, Russ Kennedy, Craig Loder, Rob Penney, Wayne Little

1993 - Flatrock Flyers

Joe Maynard (coach), Peter White, Tony Walsh, Lee Hawco, Bill Everson, Brent Sellars, Warren Sullivan, Kirby Dumaresque, Joey Maynard, Neil Maynard, Kevin Parsons, Robert Bradbury, Stephen Thornhill, Ray Bulger, Paul Shears, Derek Pelley, Ed Oates, Jack Kean, Tony Hawco, Jeff Sullivan

1994 - La Scie Jets

Gus Greco (coach), Derek Dalley, Juan Strickland, Guy Gray, Doug Ward, Neil Ward, Craig Young, Mel Best, Rob Varrin, Clint Gaudon, Roy Ward, Sheldon King, Shannon King, Monty Austins, Mark Robinson, Rob Robinson, Robert Bishop, Danny King, Lindsay Small, Blair Regular, Terry Ward, Roy Morey, Allan Critch

1995 - Southern Shore Breakers

Adrian Sullivan (coach), Denis Lake, Craig Courtney, Scott Sullivan, Bill Windsor, Jamie Coady, Andy Sullivan, Chris Davis, Ward Gosse, Jason Courtney, Barry Sullivan, Steve Scott, Gary Sullivan, Chris O'Keefe, Loyola O'Driscoll, David Walsh, Cory

Frizzell, Derek Sullivan, Keith Morey, Don Gallant, Bob Kennedy, Wade Walsh, Wayne Carew, Roger Ryan

1996 - Southern Shore Breakers

Adrian Sullivan (coach), Andy Sullivan, Scott Sullivan, Chris Davis, Loyola O'Driscoll, Ward Gosse, Jamie Tobin, Cory Frizzell, David Walsh, Roger Ryan, Aiden Maloney, Bill Windsor, Barry Sullivan, Terry Peddle, Don Roche, Brent Sullivan, Wade Duggan, Keith Morey, Gary Williams, Jason Glynn, Denis Lake, Chris O'Keefe, Jim Marnell, Derek Sullivan, Wayne Carew, Mark Aspell

1997 - Flatrock Flyers

Kev Fagan (coach), Peter White, Blair Langmead, Kirby Dumaresque, Lee Hawco, Steve Cleary, Robert Bradbury, Ed Tapper, Jack Kane, Ed Oates, Mike Evans, Al Wozney, Joey Maynard, Warren Sullivan, Ray Bulger, Tony Hawco, John Bolger, Graham Squires, Dave Goodland, Hubert Hutton, Russ Kennedy, Mike James, Kevin Parsons

1998 - Flatrock Flyers

Kevin Fagan (coach), Tony Hawco (coach), Kevin Parsons (coach), Blair Langmead, Robert Bradbury, Kirby Dumaresque, Steve Cleary, Ed Oates, Joey Maynard, Keith Maynard, Todd McDonald, Jamie Tobin, Shawn Fagan, Chris Sweet, Lee Hawco, Al Wozney, Mike James, Warren Sullivan, Todd Barron, Mike Evans, Ray Bulger, Mark Abbott

1999 - Southern Shore Breakers

Don Roche (coach), Denis Lake, Shannon Colbert, Chris O'Keefe, Brent Sullivan, Scott Sullivan, Steve Scott, Loyola O'Driscoll, Andy Sullivan, Barry Sullivan, Don Gosse, Cory Bond, Bill Windsor, Derek Sullivan, Darryl Costello, Junior Farrell, Darryl Walsh, Roger Ryan, Evan Williams, David Walsh, John O'Driscoll, Kirk Fleming

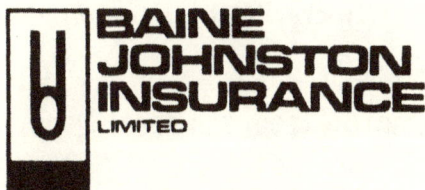

CONGRATULATIONS

on the publication of

Herder Memorial
TROPHY

the first book in

OUR SPORTS HERITAGE

FROM

BAINE JOHNSTON INSURANCE LIMITED

Ian M. Campbell, C.I.B. (NF), F.I.I.C.
PRESIDENT

10 FORT WILLIAM PLACE
ST. JOHN'S, NF A1C 5W2
(709) 576-1606

Congratulations

from

Power Hockey Programs

Boys & Girls • 5–16 years

Summer/Christmas Hockey Schools

Power Skating Programs

Newfoundland Wildcats
Elite/AAA Programs

Members of Atlantic Elite League
(Hockey Night in Boston)

(709) 579-6810 • (709) 753-7999 • (709) 368-6525

Blue|ine Sports| Inc.

Owners and Operators of
Feildian Gardens & Prince of Wales Arena

"Home of the Avalon East Hockey League"

(709) 579-9365

The Evening Telegram Winners

Year	Winner		Year	Winner
1954	Bell Island		1977	Corner Brook
1955	Bell Island		1978	Blue Caps
1956	Bell Island		1979	Gander
1957	Grand Falls		1980	Gander
1958	Grand Falls		1981	Grand Falls
1959	Grand Falls		1982	Gander
1960	Not awarded		1983	Stephenville
1961	Not awarded		1984	Stephenville
1962	Conception Bay		1985	Stephenville
1963	Buchans		1986	Stephenville
1964	Corner Brook		1987	St. John's
1965	Conception Bay		1988	St. John's
1966	Corner Brook		1989	St. John's
1967	Gander		1990	Not awarded
1968	Grand Falls		1991	Not awarded
1969	Gander		1992	Not awarded
1970	St. John's		1993	Bell Island
1971	St. John's		1994	Southern Shore
1972	Grand Falls		1995	Southern Shore
1973	Corner Brook		1996	St. John's
1974	St. John's		1997	Flatrock
1975	St. John's		1998	Southern Shore
1976	St. John's		1999	Badger

Congratulations

on the publication of

OUR SPORTS HERITAGE

from

B & W Auto Repairs
Mount Pearl Ultramar

Self Serve & Full Serve Gasoline
General Car Repairs

Commonwealth Avenue
(709) 368-8962

Top Scorers

1963	Mike Kelly	Buchans	40
1964	Don Barrett	Buchans	63
1965	Alex Faulkner	CeeBees	79
1966	Mike Kelly	Gander	91
1967	Mike Kelly	Gander	92
1968	Jacques Allard	Gander	131
1969	Jacques Allard	Gander	126
1970	Frank Dorrington	Corner Brook	118
1971	Jack Faulkner	Gander	74
1972	Wayne Maxner	Gander	111
1973	Frank Dorrington	Corner Brook	67
1974	Frank Dorrington	Corner Brook	101
1975	Charlie Greene	Grand Falls	46
1976	Gene Faulkner	Grand Falls	39
1977	Denis Goulding	Gander	91
1978	Randy Pearcey	Blue Caps	106
1979	Ed Philpott	Gander	126
1980	Zane Forbes	Gander	94
1981	Randy Pearcey	Blue Caps	86
1982	Bruce Campbell	Grand Falls	75
1983	Bruce Campbell	Stephenville	73
1984	Juan Strickland	Port aux Basques	92
1985	Juan Strickland	Port aux Basques	88
1986	Robbie Forbes	Corner Brook	117
1987	Andy Sullivan	St. John's	130
1988	Craig Jenkins	Corner Brook	157
1989	Andy Sullivan	St. John's	106
1990	Not awarded		
1991	Not awarded		
1992	Not awarded		
1993	Andy Sullivan	Pouch Cove	63
1994	Andy Sullivan	Southern Shore	49
1995	Andy Sullivan	Southern Shore	100
1996	Denis Strong	CeeBees	59
1997	Derek Dalley	Twillingate	45
1998	Scott Sullivan	Southern Shore	117
1999	Ed Russell	Conception Bay	71

Congratulations

to

BREAKWATER

on the publication

of

Herder Memorial TROPHY

from

Byron's
Clothing For Men

190 Water St. • (709) 753-5555

Top Goaltenders

1963	Bill Sullivan	CeeBees	4.31
1964	Bert Brake	Corner Brook	3.35
1965	Terry Matthews	CeeBees	3.50
1966	Bert Brake	Corner Brook	4.29
1967	Lyle Carter	Gander	3.89
1968	Fred Janes	Grand Falls	3.90
1969	Fred Janes	Grand Falls	3.70
1970	Eg Billard	St. John's	3.80
1971	Eg Billard	St. John's	3.94
1972	J. G. Morrissette	Grand Falls	2.33
1973	Rocky Martin	Grand Falls	4.14
1974	Tols Chapman	St. John's	3.53
1975	Tols Chapman	St. John's	2.63
1976	Pat Dempsey	St. John's	3.11
1977	Ted McComb	Corner Brook	3.76
1978	Pat Dempsey	St. John's	3.71
1979	Pat Dempsey	St. John's	4.02
1980	Kevin Kelly	Gander	3.55
1981	Roger Kennedy	St. John's	4.36
1982	Ed Davis	Grand Falls	4.02
1983	Gary Dunville	Stephenville	3.33
1984	Gary Dunville	Stephenville	3.64
1985	Gary Dunville	Stephenville	3.52
1986	Dave Matte	Corner Brook	3.75
1987	Peter White	St. John's	3.39
1988	Roger Kennedy	St. John's	3.85
1989	Roger Kennedy	St. John's	4.78
1990	Not awarded		
1991	Not awarded		
1992	Not awarded		
1993	Roger Kennedy	Badger	3.13
1994	Roger Kennedy	Badger	3.77
1995	Peter White	Flatrock	1.58
1996	Blair Langmead	Flatrock	1.75
1997	Peter White	Flatrock	2.00
1998	Blair Langmead	Flatrock	0.92
1999	Blair Langmead	Flatrock	1.92

Proud Supporter

of

OUR SPORTS HERITAGE

THAT PRO LOOK

"1st Choice in Sports Apparel"

New Location

Lower Level, Avalon Mall

Tel: (709) 739-5665   Fax: (709) 753-5491

Rookies
of the Year

1969	Terry French	Grand Falls
1970	Bruce Butler	St. John's
	Cliff Piercey	Buchans
1971	Bram Pike	Corner Brook
1972	Don Howse	Grand Falls
1973	Gary Connolly	St. John's
1974	Dave Oxford	Corner Brook
1975	Glen Critch	St. John's
1976	Cal Dunville	Stephenville
1977	Erik Seaward	Memorial University
1978	Zane Forbes	Gander
1979	John Breen	Shamrocks
1980	Mac Tucker	Blue Caps
1981	Roger Kennedy	St. John's
1982	Jim Mercer	Gander
1983	Juan Strickland	Stephenville
1984	Rob Brown	Corner Brook
1985	Kev McCarthy	Corner Brook
1986	Ken Mercer	Corner Brook
1987	Peter White	St. John's
1988	Derek Dalley	Gander
1989	Brent Jenkins	Corner Brook
1990	Not awarded	
1991	Not awarded	
1992	Not awarded	
1993	Bill Williams	Bell Island
1994	Kevin Fitzpatrick	Torbay
1995	Trevor Boland	Outer Cove
1996	Devon Penney	Bell Island
1997	Jamie Tobin	Southern Shore
1998	Mark Robinson	Conception Bay
1999	Ed Russell	Conception Bay

Proud Sponsor

of

OUR SPORTS HERITAGE

Centennial Sports Bar

Mount Pearl's #1 Sports Bar

46 Bannister Street
(709) 368-2909

F

Most Gentlemanly Players

1974	Al Dwyer	Grand Falls
1975	Al Dwyer	Grand Falls
1976	Hubert Hutton	St. John's
1977	Tom Rafuse	Gander
1978	Ted Mercer	Gander
1979	Ed Philpott	Gander
1980	Tom Rafuse	Gander
1981	Dan Flynn	Grand Falls
1982	Bruce Campbell	Grand Falls
1983	Juan Strickland	Stephenville
1984	Wayne Dove	Stephenville
1985	Andy Sullivan	Stephenville
1986	Andy Sullivan	Stephenville
1987	Robbie Forbes	Corner Brook
1988	Craig Jenkins	Corner Brook
1989	Darren McWhirter	Corner Brook
1990	Not awarded	
1991	Not awarded	
1992	Not awarded	
1993	Russ Kennedy	Badger
1994	Derek Dalley	La Scie
1995	Robert Bradbury	Flatrock
1996	Devon Penney	Bell Island
1997	Bill Windsor	Southern Shore
1998	Robert Bradbury	Flatrock
1999	Brent Sullivan	Southern Shore

Most Valuable Players

1981	Bruce Campbell	Corner Brook
1982	Zane Forbes	Gander
1983	Roger Kennedy	St. John's
1984	Gary Dunville	Stephenville
1985	Zane Forbes	Stephenville
1986	Dave Matte	Corner Brook
1987	Andy Sullivan	St. John's
1988	Dan Cormier	Corner Brook
1989	Marc West	Port aux Basques
1990	Not awarded	
1991	Not awarded	
1992	Not awarded	
1993	Andy Sullivan	Pouch Cove
1994	Bill Bishop	Portugal Cove
1995	Bill Windsor	Southern Shore
1996	Kevin Fitzpatrick	Torbay
1997	Kirby Dumaresque	Flatrock
1998	Scott Sullivan	Southern Shore
1999	Steve Mifflin	Conception Bay Central

MacCormack
TROPHY

The major battles for the senior baseball championship have featured St. John's, Grand Falls and Corner Brook baseball teams. The first winner was declared in 1948 and the competition has been just as intense during the past 50 years. The second book in the series takes a look at the many great players that have performed in the senior leagues.

Available June 2000 • $14.95

Challenge
CUP

Soccer has long been one of the great past-times in Newfoundland and Labrador and the competition for the Canadian Challenge Cup has brought provincial soccer to greater heights. The contribution of players from the Burin Peninsula has maintained soccer as one of the most popular sports in the province. The third book in the series profiles the Challenge Cup competition and the great players that have performed for the provincial title.

Available October 2000 • $14.95

www.ingramcontent.com/pod-product-compliance
Lightning Source LLC
LaVergne TN
LVHW011234080426
835509LV00005B/490